Start Your Own

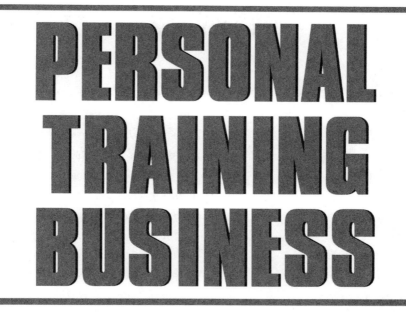

PERSONAL TRAINING BUSINESS

Additional titles in *Entrepreneur's* Startup Series

Start Your Own

Entrepreneur
MAGAZINE'S

start*up*

3RD EDITION

Start Your Own

PERSONAL TRAINING BUSINESS

Your Step-by-Step Guide to Success

Entrepreneur Press and Ciree Linsenman

EP
Entrepreneur.
Press

Entrepreneur Press, Publisher
Cover Design: Beth Hansen-Winter
Production and Composition: Eliot House Productions

This publication is designed to provide accurate and authoritative information in regard
to the subject matter covered. It is sold with the understanding that the publisher is not
engaged in rendering legal, accounting or other professional services. If legal advice or
other expert assistance is required, the services of a competent professional person should
be sought.

Library of Congress Cataloging-in-Publication Data
Linsenman, Ciree.
    Start your own personal training business/by Entrepreneur Press and Ciree
Linsenman.—3rd ed.
      p.   cm.
    Includes index.
    ISBN-13: 978-1-59918-426-5 (alk. paper)
    ISBN–10: 1-59918-426-5 (alk. paper)
    1. Personal trainers. 2. Physical education and training. I. Title.
GV428.7.L95 2012
613.7'1—dc23   2012000892

Printed in the United States of America

16 15 14 13 12   10 9 8 7 6 5 4 3 2 1

Contents

▲

Preface

Almost every day, it seems, there is a major story in the popular media that focuses on health and fitness. From breakthrough nutrition research to tips on starting a walking program to advice on improving flexibility, the coverage reaches literally millions of people through newspapers, magazines, books, websites, and TV shows.

Yet, the same popular media frequently reports about the obesity problem. The familiar numbers are heard so often that the shock value is wearing off: More than a third of U.S. adults are considered obese, while another third are considered overweight. All told, those statistics encompass a population of more than 190 million people.

It's a great paradox—with all we know about healthy living, why are many people still struggling to get in shape?

Maybe there is just too much information and people are overwhelmed. Or perhaps they lack the motivation necessary to carry through on a fitness program. Whatever the reason, as a personal trainer you have both a great opportunity and a significant challenge. You are in demand to help people not just wade through all of the information, but to inspire them to apply it and improve their lives.

As a result, starting a personal training business offers a satisfying combination of financial reward and a career in which you can make a profound difference in the lives of others. A skilled trainer who also has good business knowledge and judgment can earn a substantial income.

At the same time, because many people still face troubling weight and healthy lifestyle issues, new approaches are needed if fitness professionals are to reach these individuals.

Fortunately, the fitness business is rising to the challenge by creating innovative ways to do just that. This means that you have new avenues to entrepreneurial success through strategies that will grow your business by making fitness relevant and accessible for more and more people.

In this updated edition, we give you information that will quickly get you up to speed on these exciting directions in the fitness industry and show you how you can take advantage of them. You'll see, for example, how the emerging field of wellness coaching is using important discoveries in behavior modification to access the powerful internal motivations of clients. You'll also learn how Zumba, boot camps, and using outdoor, picturesque venues are satisfying growing social needs and the desire for more affordable fitness options. Also, we cover how trainers are eschewing a one-size-fits-all approach and targeting their training services toward the specific needs of particular populations, such as youth or older adults. We explain how fitness organizations also are responding by offering specialized certifications or continuing education that better prepares trainers to address the needs of particular segments of clients.

What's more, we describe how functional training is being used to help sedentary clients better perform the tasks of everyday living. A personal trainer today must be well-versed in the theories behind functional training—trust us, your competitors will be. More importantly, trainers must know how to put theory into practice and deliver effective and safe functional workouts to clients.

This third edition also includes expanded information on how using the full potential that social media has to offer can revolutionize your business. Having a website is almost mandatory and will give you instant credibility, no matter what the size of your company. We explain how you can bring your business into cyberspace, either by creating a simple website that acts as an electronic brochure for your training business or by setting up a site that allows you to train clients online. But beyond a basic website, and potentially more importantly, we'll walk you through how to create a social media presence in a variety of venues, in simplified steps.

As with the second and first editions, this book generally focuses on the business side of personal training. This is not an instruction book on training techniques—there are plenty of certification and education programs where you can find that.

But we realize that you're interested in exercise, athletic performance, and how science is exploring ways that we can become fitter and healthier. You wouldn't be a personal trainer or a soon-to-be trainer if you weren't. So we've added sidebars throughout the book giving you "Stat Facts"—you'll find these fascinating, we're sure. But they're also perfect tidbits of information that you can pass along to your clients to enhance your reputation as a reliable source of health and fitness knowledge.

This book also covers the nitty-gritty details of starting and running a successful fitness business. Whether you're looking to launch a solo concern with minimal investment or open your own studio and hire other trainers, this book will help you. You'll get an overview of the industry and potential client markets, as well as a step-by-step guide to setting up and operating your fitness business. You'll learn about startup costs, marketing, and how to track and manage your company's finances. Successful personal trainers and industry experts will share the insights they've gained through years of experience.

Regardless of the type of personal training business you want to start, we recommend that you read every chapter in this book. Most of the information applies to all sizes and types of personal training operations, and the information is interrelated.

Introduction to Personal Training

This is an exciting time to be an entrepreneurial personal trainer. The opportunities for qualified fitness professionals who also understand how to run a business are virtually unlimited.

Take a look around. Obesity is an epidemic. Many people of all ages are spending too much time in front of computers and

TVs, and this increasingly sedentary lifestyle is taking a tremendous toll on their health. Fast-food restaurants serve up calorie-dense meals and regular restaurants offer massive portion sizes.

As people decide to do something about their expanding waistlines and finally get in shape, fitness professionals are well-positioned to help. Whether the market is baby boomers wanting to regain some of their youthful vitality or parents looking for ways to provide positive role models for their children, they are turning to trainers. As well, doctors and managed care organizations have recognized that diet and exercise are an important part of keeping people healthy and avoiding unnecessary health-care costs. Even companies are realizing that healthy, fit employees are more productive.

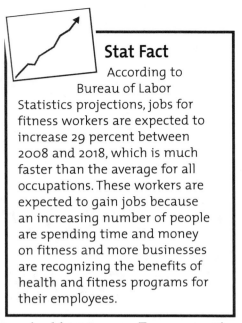

Stat Fact
According to Bureau of Labor Statistics projections, jobs for fitness workers are expected to increase 29 percent between 2008 and 2018, which is much faster than the average for all occupations. These workers are expected to gain jobs because an increasing number of people are spending time and money on fitness and more businesses are recognizing the benefits of health and fitness programs for their employees.

It's no surprise that personal training is one of the top professions of the 21st century and a fast-growing segment of the fitness industry. With rare exceptions, personal trainers love what they do. After all, they're not working on a production line or sitting in front of a computer—they're helping people get and stay healthy and fit. For their efforts, they're earning $40 to $150 or more per hour.

"The industry is continuing to grow," says Tony Ordas, former director of certification for the American Council on Exercise (ACE). "There has been a steady increase in growth in the number of health and fitness facilities. More and more clubs are in dire need of personal trainers." While some of those clubs want their trainers to work as employees, many others are hiring independent contractors or contracting with personal training companies to meet their needs—and that means opportunity for you.

What Do Personal Trainers Do?

Personal trainers work with clients who need instruction and coaching in the areas of exercise physiology, kinesiology, injury prevention, recovery and rehabilitation, nutrition, supplementation, fitness assessment, exercise programming, sports conditioning, flexibility techniques, and more. Personal trainers used to more often train individuals one-on-one, but today group instruction is gaining ground because of the multiple benefits to both trainer and trainee, including sociability, learning from peers as well as instructors, and typically lower rate structures.

Observant, detail-oriented personal trainers begin their work with each client by doing an assessment. Through conversation and by completing forms, they gather information about the client's health and medical status, lifestyle, expectations, and preferences. Then they are able to establish realistic and measurable short- and long-term goals and develop an exercise program. Some trainers set up a series of short-term goals that the client can strive for, and others space the rewards out at greater intervals, coaching clients to reach for the ultimate brass ring and then its maintenance. The choice is yours to make, but one thing is clear: A high emotional IQ, an understanding of basic "people skills" and psychology, and the desire to help people are all needed to process the subtle but important signals your clients may give you along the way.

Personal trainer Salvador Mascarenas Ruiz of Puerto Vallarta, Mexico, believes being a good teacher is in one's genes and unless you take pleasure from sharing what you know and have an innate love of giving versus taking, working as a fitness trainer will be painful for everyone involved, both student and teacher. Phil Martens of 501F1T in Minneapolis, Minnesota, says "Your best bet for success is to be able to connect with people, to respect them, and really know your program and what you're doing. A high emotional IQ would be good, but really a Ph.D. in psychology would be even better."

As they work with each client, personal trainers teach safe and effective exercise techniques; they monitor, record, and evaluate progress; they make adjustments in the program as necessary; and they provide support and motivation to help their

Every Stripe and Shape

So what do personal trainers really do? Some of the services typically offered by personal trainers include:

- ○ Body composition and fitness assessments
- ○ Muscle building and toning
- ○ Boot camps
- ○ Group dance sessions
- ○ Individual exercise programs
- ○ Individual weight/fat-loss programs
- ○ Nutrition consulting (in conjunction with a licensed nutritionist)
- ○ Strength and endurance training
- ○ In-home or in-office personal training
- ○ Home gym development
- ○ Personal training for teenagers and children
- ○ Personal training for seniors
- ○ Clinical exercise
- ○ Sports conditioning
- ○ Wellness coaching
- ○ Stress management programs
- ○ Special focus training such as cardio-respiratory, circuit, and resistance
- ○ Flexibility exercises
- ○ Individually designed high- or low-impact step and aerobics programs
- ○ Individual or small group training
- ○ Seminars and classes on fitness

clients stick to the program and reach their goals. Personal trainers may also serve as consultants when their clients are setting up training equipment in their homes or offices.

Personal trainers who have studied nutrition may also offer nutrition and weight management counseling. Trainers who are group fitness instructors may incorporate popular group fitness trends into small group training sessions. For example, your clients may not want to participate in a crowded class at the gym but may want you to lead very small classes in areas such as yoga, kickboxing, zumba, and body sculpting for themselves, their families, and friends.

Some personal trainers work with people who have suffered an illness or injury and need assistance transitioning back to a physically active lifestyle. This is an area known as "clinical exercise" and is an important part of the rehabilitation process. Trainers work in conjunction with their clients' medical doctors and physical therapists to establish an appropriate exercise program; then they instruct the client as necessary to implement the program.

Trainers work with amateur and professional athletes to help them maintain their conditioning during their off season and prepare for in-season competition. They work with performers who may or may not be celebrities, but who need to stay in top physical form or get back into shape quickly for an event.

Three Timeless Questions

The 2009 "Future of Fitness White Paper" published by Les Mills International asks perhaps the three most important questions relevant to success in the fitness industry. Keep these questions in mind when you shape and refine your business.

1. How do we remain relevant among the "converted" consumers—those who already believe in fitness and are willing to commit time and effort?

2. Can we improve our offer to those who enjoy fitness, but who don't like "going to the gym"?

3. How do we keep the industry fresh, relevant, and competitive in the decades ahead as populations change, technology and medicine redefine what is possible, and competition increases?

Stay tuned throughout the book for the data these questions unearthed, and view the study here: www.futureoffitnesswhitepaper.com.

Meet the Experts

Personal trainers today expand their services and then refine them, specializing not just in what their markets call for but also what stimulates personal growth. Some of the trainers interviewed in this book have switched gears several times for those reasons. In our panel you'll find a balanced sample of current trends as well as traditional methods.

Jennifer Brilliant's Brooklyn-based company offers one-on-one training, as well as group training in exercise and yoga. Jennifer and her trainers work in homes, offices, schools, and gyms.

Lynne Wells, in New York City, works with clients in their homes and in the gyms located in residential buildings where the clients live.

Bill Sonnemaker owns Catalyst Fitness in the Atlanta area, and employs three full-time and two part-time trainers. He's the recipient of the 2007 IDEA International Personal Trainer of the Year Award and the 2007 National Academy of Sports Medicine Pursuit of Excellence in Health and Fitness Award. One of the keys to his success, he says, is his time as an intern and employee of other trainers. "I had access to good coaches with good exercise technique, and learned proper form and proper program design," he says.

Gunnar Peterson has had a lifetime to refine the powerful style that makes him one of the most talked-about personal trainers for those striving for strength, health, and beauty. From age 10 he began the discovery of how to change his own body from fat to fit, beginning with joining Weight Watchers. He fell in love with the feeling of empowerment and being able to change his body and since has kept his passion candle lit to give others the tools to reach their personal health

Gunnar Peterson on the rings

goals through a distinctive, unconventional style that attracts professional athletes, everyday people, and celebrities.

Running his Beverly Hills, California, gym and being a single parent to kids Sloan, age 7, Jack, age 12, and Henry, age 13, requires an intense level of energy, which Peterson is known for, along with the sarcastic sense of humor he's used for over 20 years to hold clients accountable for changing their own lives.

Peterson's Strength and Conditioning Specialist (CSCS) certification and fluid transfer of strength training modalities from gym use to home and office cubicle use are just some of the implements that make him so useful. He enables progress for professional athletes and office workers alike, giving them the tools they need to work realistically within the confines of their unique schedules.

Tyrone Minor started out as a division one track athlete in college and competed nationally until he was 33. As he traveled to compete, he networked with local athletes to find the best gyms in each city and began getting requests for training assistance. A light bulb went off as more fitness buffs asked to train with him.

Research and development of his own personal training business came next, along with the beginnings of his intense coaching style, a combination of offering "confuse the body" exercise sets, working the largest muscle groups to lose fat and gain mass, and functional compound movements designed to help people do daily life tasks with more strength and stability.

He is a licensed physical education teacher and registered trainer, and doubles as a fitness model for a variety of product lines. His personal training business, Chizel Inc., is in Minneapolis, Minnesota.

Having sailed solo around the world on a 31-foot cutter boat at age 57, Pat Henry discovered and honed the physical and emotional strengths that saw her through most every challenge imaginable. The rigors of that eight-year adventure combined with wear-and-tear to her body from years of competitive athletics and aging heightened her awareness of and interest in the relationship between anatomical mechanics and physical injuries.

She immersed herself in studying and became a certified pain management therapist. She utilized the pain management principles to develop a unique program: Organic Stretching™. Traditionally, therapy serves clients in addressing their individual restrictions and the potential benefits are dependent upon the practitioner doing the work. Henry was determined to give clients the tools to heal themselves and strengthen their physical wellness by teaching them how to move. She practices in Nayarit, Mexico, and Laredo, Texas.

501F1T is a socially energized fitness center in Minneapolis, Minnesota. This partnership of Phil Martens and Diana Broschka offers clients long-term, affordable group fitness classes and personal training with both traditional and custom equipment designed by Martens.

When the partnership began, Martens was running a solo training business with a small client base. Keeping the business small allowed him to work a 30-hour week and close the studio gym he rented when he didn't have clients to work on marketing his business. He began to develop a fitness machine called G-Werx Gym™ and expand, and needed a business plan. Diana Broschka, one of Martens' clients, believed in him and though she'd never written one, offered to write it for him.

With Broschka's impressive resume in finance and business and Martens' law degree and inventor status, the dynamo began kicking up dust soon after the plan gelled, and today they are starting to enjoy some of the payoffs of being extremely diligent for three years in the creation of the multiple projects surrounding their gym.

In the Mexican border town of Reynosa, Tamaulipas, being overweight was a positive, indicating one had sufficient funds to eat heartily. A painful lesson came for young, hefty Salvador Mascarenas Ruiz when his family moved to Monterrey, one of Mexico's most developed and prosperous metropolises. There his girth was grist for ridicule and exclusion. In response to the cruel teasing he began running and virtually stopped eating, consuming only one salad every other day. He lost a lot of weight very quickly and became ill from the process.

Treating him with antibiotics, the attending physician also gave Mascarenas Ruiz books on how to eat nutritionally and safely attain a healthy weight. One in particular, written in a comic book style, had a life-changing impact: *La Panza es Primero* (*The Belly Is First*) by Ruis, an author who uses no first name (not to be confused with Mascarena Ruiz). Its message that good nutrition is the cornerstone of wellness was told with humor and emphasizes minimizing meat, fat, and sugar. Ruiz was forever changed and began his education in health and fitness.

Applying this newly acquired nutritional wisdom and developing his personal fitness through sampling various exercise forms, Mascarenas Ruiz over time not only restored his health but achieved an exemplary physique, which brought plentiful opportunities for modeling and acting.

"I can do that!" is the mantra that not only launched Barbara Crompton's comprehensive fitness career more than three decades ago but has also served to guide her professional development and business decisions along the way. Inspired by a class at the Jane Fonda Center in Los Angeles, California, she decided to apply her university degree in physical education to developing her own aerobics, stretch, and strength classes. She initially found willing participants in her family and friends, and with the blind optimism of youth and an unflagging work ethic earned Canadian and international certifications in various fitness disciplines.

Her ventures soon after included founding and directing several fitness enterprises, such as a personal training company employing 22 trainers, a physical therapy and massage clinic for injured athletes, and a fitness educators' business that provided international training for health professionals and all-inclusive resources to assist in the opening and on-going management of private and corporate fitness centers.

Personal trainers are not simply exercise instructors and supervisors—in other words, there's more to being a personal trainer than just knowing your anatomy and exercise physiology and the sciences behind exercise. Each of the experts in this book came to serve the human race with a specialized form of physical assistance because of a fondness for empowering people, their own struggles attaining peak fitness, and a gift for helping to heal. The personal experiences that led to commit deeply to such a disciplined and industrious lifestyle have been emotional and character-building. As a result of this hard-won experience trainers have the potential to be skilled and sensitive confidants, role models, and sources of support and encouragement.

They are engaged, invested, and giving, and want to see their clients soar to their highest potential. Of course, when you turn your life's passion into a business, you'll have to be proficient at much more than that. In the beginning, you may choose to take on all of the management elements of your business yourself. You'll handle everything from marketing, selling, and social media representation to accounting and employee relations.

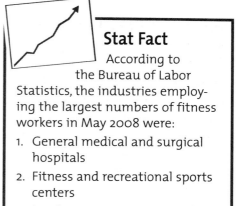

Stat Fact
According to the Bureau of Labor Statistics, the industries employing the largest numbers of fitness workers in May 2008 were:

1. General medical and surgical hospitals
2. Fitness and recreational sports centers
3. Local government, civic, and social organizations
4. Schools and training facilities

Who Is Your Market?

Successful personal trainers agree that there is no such thing as a "typical" client. More and more people, regardless of their level of fitness or exercise expertise, are turning to personal trainers as a practical and affordable means of becoming and staying healthy. Hard-core strength trainers and body builders are only part of the overall clientele of personal trainers.

Pat Henry's Organic Stretching™ helps clientele ranging in age from 45 to 80, many of whom have experienced significant improvement with long-term and episodic lower back, shoulder, knee, and sciatica issues. The entire focus of Henry's method is on increasing range of motion relying on using connective tissue, especially the joints, which is an asset to anyone, regardless of their exercise regimen or fitness level.

Jennifer Brilliant's clients include businesspeople, stay-at-home mothers, and people recovering from injuries and illnesses. "Some people are striving to get into better shape, whatever that means for them," she says. "Some are into maintenance, so they're not really trying to improve; they just want to stay where they are. Some people want to learn something new for variety."

How long do clients typically stay with a personal trainer? It can range from just a few sessions to years. Some trainers carefully seek out long-term clients; others choose a niche where they educate a client about fitness, or work them through a short-term problem, then move on. Brilliant says her clients stay with her an average of three to five years. Phil Martens still has some of the same clients from the small gym he operated seven years ago.

Snowbirds, Expatriates, and Sensuality

Choosing to serve somewhat of a snowbird crowd—as do Pat Henry, Barbara Crompton, and Salvador Mascarenas Ruiz—creates a rewarding balancing act to master. Many communities like Puerto Vallarta attract a mix of expatriates from all over the world, many of whom choose to keep two residences, one in their vacation spot, and the other in their hometown. This creates an opportunity for personal trainers to capitalize on the very reasons this market creates that "of the body" lifestyle. The visitors look to rejuvenate, become robust, regain beauty, try new forms of creative expression that they dare not in their hometown, and learn how to simply enjoy life again.

To call places like Puerto Vallarta "tourist venues" is not entirely accurate, for many visitors consider themselves residents and take their halftime status to heart, using all the amenities the venues offer to recuperate and prepare for their more serious, industrious lives elsewhere. From cosmetic surgery and total-body overhauls to playing in whatever art form they choose, places like Puerto Vallarta more often than not offer it cheaper and with more anonymity than buyers can get at home. With money for indulgences and a mission to become the person they always wanted to be, this crowd is ripe for personal trainers of all types.

Some trainers work with people who travel frequently so the relationship is as long as ten years, but the sessions may only occur two or three months of the year. Some clients want frequent sessions with their trainers—as many as two and three a week. Others opt to see their trainers less often, perhaps just to do periodic fitness testing, measure their progress, and update their program. Lynne Wells says she typically sees her clients one to three times a week, and most have been with her for more than three years.

Realize that not everyone who has an interest in fitness is a potential client; many dedicated fitness buffs prefer to do their own thing. Along the same line, not everyone who needs a personal trainer is going to be willing and/or able to hire one.

Is This Business for You?

There are two key aspects to owning a personal training business. The first is being a personal trainer, and the second is being an entrepreneur.

Good personal trainers are passionate about fitness and eager to learn the latest information about exercise, nutrition, and healthy lifestyles. They enjoy helping and teaching others about fitness and exercise. They are caring, giving, patient, and empathetic. They absolutely love the idea of spending ten hours per day working with people in a gym or other setting, guiding them through exercises, and helping them reach their fitness goals.

As a trainer, your job is to motivate your clients, improve their techniques, and keep their workouts fun and effective. You need to be friendly, enthusiastic, and have great communication skills to do this. It also helps to be personable, genuine, and truly sincere—you're not trying to sell anything; you're helping people, and for that, you get paid.

Successful entrepreneurs have the ability to step beyond doing the service their company offers and deal with the process of building and running a business. To own

Bright Idea

In the 2009 "Future of Fitness White Paper" published by Les Mills International, we see the rapid delivery of technology affecting the expectations people have of their fitness results. Predictions from the white paper include consumer demand for customized services that cater to their circumstances, such as a virtual personal trainer program to lead their home workouts, a link that lets them join their gym group from home, or virtual experiences with other activities such as experiencing a jog through the park as a science fiction adventure. Read more at: www.lesmills.com.

your own personal training business, you'll need strong management, administrative, and marketing skills—or you'll need to recognize what you don't have and then cultivate them in yourself or be willing to hire people who can provide those skills.

As Bill Sonnemaker says, "Being good at your job as a trainer is completely different than being a good marketer or good business owner . . . so finding your strengths and weaknesses is important."

Jennifer Brilliant was a dancer for many years before she became a personal trainer. For her, the appeal of personal training was "sharing and helping others." Jennifer says, "It's a profession where people are giving, and with that generosity, people are successful." But she knows she has to do more than just work with clients. "The part of the business that's challenging is the day-to-day things you have to do, all the details of running a business—the bookkeeping, handling phone calls, keeping records straight," she says. "It's surprising how much time running the business takes."

Credibility and Credentials

There are no professional licensing requirements for personal trainers. That means anyone can call himself a personal trainer and open up a business. But consumers are becoming increasingly savvy, and most will ask about your credentials before they hire you. That's why certifications and professional affiliations are critical.

"The big difference between licensure and certification is that certification is voluntary, whereas licensure is mandated by the state," says Tony Ordas. "Certification is a credential that states you have a certain level of knowledge and skill."

There may be more than 300 organizations offering certification programs—some general, others very specialized—for personal trainers (although it doesn't appear that anyone keeps an official count). Most are for-profit, but a few are nonprofit. The majority of these organizations also offer education programs leading to certification, although several merely administer tests to determine competency. Some of the education and certification organizations also function like a professional association, providing individuals who have completed their programs with a range of ongoing support services. There are also professional associations, which are just that—an association of personal trainers and

Tip...

Smart Tip

Even though certification is not required at present, it's always possible that legislation requiring some sort of licensure or certification could be passed in any state at any time. If that happens and you're not certified, you're out of business. So get certified. Insist that the trainers who work for you be certified as well.

It's Official!

Some of the certifications you might want to consider obtaining include:

- ○ Aerobic Fitness Trainer
- ○ Aqua Fitness Specialist
- ○ Certified Fitness Advisor
- ○ Certified Personal Trainer
- ○ Clinical Exercise Specialist
- ○ First Responder/First Aid
- ○ Fitness Therapist
- ○ Golf Fitness Trainer
- ○ Group Fitness Instructor
- ○ Health Fitness Instructor
- ○ Lifestyle and Weight Management Consultant
- ○ Neonatal/Postpartum Exercise Specialist
- ○ Wellness Coach
- ○ Performance Nutrition Specialist
- ○ Personal Defense Specialist
- ○ Rehabilitation Exercise Specialist
- ○ Senior Fitness Specialist
- ○ Specialist in Fitness for the Physically Limited
- ○ Specialist in Martial Art Conditioning
- ○ Sports Conditioning Specialist
- ○ Strength and Conditioning Specialist
- ○ Water Fitness Trainer
- ○ Youth Fitness Trainer
- ○ Zumba Instructor

other fitness professionals. A number of these organizations are listed in the Appendix; you can find even more by doing a search on the internet or visiting your local library.

With such an abundance of choices, it makes sense to recognize that you can't belong to every fitness organization out there. That's an expensive and counterproductive approach. Study the organizations and choose the one(s) that meet your requirements and will give you the tools you need to succeed.

When deciding on the organization(s) you'll work with to obtain your credentials, consider these issues:

- *Accreditation*. Check to see if the certifying organization is accredited, and by whom. It's a good idea to also check into the accreditation agency to determine how they set standards and what sort of reputation they have. Although there are hundreds of personal training certification organizations, only a handful of nationally recognized organizations are accredited by the National Commission for Certifying Agencies. This is the accreditation body of National Organization for Competency Assurance, which sets quality standards for credentialing organizations.

- *Club requirements*. If you are going to contract with a club or spa to provide their personal training services, they may require that you and the trainers on your staff be certified through specific organizations. Find out what they prefer before investing in a program they won't accept.

- *Your goals*. Be sure the certification is something you can use and is in line with the goals and aspirations you have for yourself and your company.

- *Your market*. The certification should be appropriate for the market segment you want to serve.

- *The current fitness forecast of leading authorities*. Check to see which fitness niches are on their way in and which are on their way out with the research.

- *Your educational needs*. Some certifying organizations offer only testing programs that determine skills and competency; others offer training programs that lead to certification. Your own needs will determine which you choose. For more information on how to evaluate a certification organization, see Chapter 8.

Beyond industry-related certification, many personal trainers have college degrees in health/exercise sciences or related fields. These degrees demonstrate your knowledge and commitment to the field.

A sampling of some of the trainers we interviewed reveals the value they place on maintaining qualifications. In addition to two certifications from the American Council on Exercise (ACE), Jennifer B. also holds a fine arts degree in dance. Bill S.'s credentials include work as a research chemist for the Centers for Disease Control and

Prevention, a pending master's degree in exercise science, and certifications through the National Academy of Sports Medicine, the National Strength and Conditioning Association, the American College of Sports Medicine (ACSM), and ACE. Lynne Wells is certified through ACE, has a certification in lifestyle and weight management consulting, and two certifications in Hatha yoga.

Richard Cotton holds a certification through ACSM, as well as a master's degree in physical education with an emphasis in applied exercise science. If you choose to pursue a degree, Cotton says, "physical education, kinesiology, and exercise physiology (all with an applied emphasis as opposed to research emphasis)" are helpful courses of study for this field.

> ## Dollar Stretcher
>
> If you live near a medical school, take advantage of their medical libraries, which contain textbooks and journals that are more expensive to buy or subscribe to than most personal trainers can afford. These are your best sources for timely, accurate information. You should also check out www.pubmed.com, which allows you to search academic journals based on key words—abstracts are free, and many journals are now making full-text articles free, as well (some require a delay of up to a year after publication before giving free access).

Phil Martens is an ACE Certified Trainer with a bachelor's and a doctorate degree from the University of Minnesota.

In addition to being a certified trainer and licensed educator, Tyrone Minor has a Master of Education degree in applied kinesiology and an M.A. in sports management.

Barbara Crompton's educational focus in physiology and anatomy offers a confident structure to her holistic services.

Continuing Education

Once you receive a certification, the organization will likely require you to earn continuing education units (CEUs) on a periodic basis to maintain that credential. Most offer a wide range of classes and seminars for a fee, so it's easy to choose sessions that are of interest and appropriate for your particular operation. Before signing up for a class, be sure to confirm how many CEUs you'll earn and what sort of documentation is required to be sure you get proper credit.

Whether it's required or not, you should always be educating yourself on the latest trends and discoveries in the fitness industry. New products and techniques are constantly being introduced, and you should be familiar with them so you know when to use them with your clients. In fact, a great place to take seminars is at the various trade shows and conventions where equipment vendors are displaying their products.

▲

Sound Off on Your Certifications

Atlanta-based Bill Sonnemaker requires each of his trainers to eventually obtain certifications from four of the top organizations: the National Academy of Sports Medicine, the American College of Sports Medicine, the American Council on Exercise, and the National Strength and Conditioning Association. "All of our trainers have at least two of those to begin to work with clients," he says. "This requirement is just so far above any other facility that we advertise on that."

Also, your clients may hear about various fitness-related issues in the media, and you need to be prepared to answer their questions with confidence and accuracy.

Remember that your certifications and the continuing education necessary to maintain them underpin your business success. "The knowledge I've obtained while preparing for certification exams," Sonnemaker says "as well as the teaching and education required to maintain those certifications, has made me a better trainer when it comes to assessments, program design, and psychological factors in dealing with clients."

"When you work with athletes you need to keep up-to-date on the latest training philosophies," says Tyrone Minor of Chizel Inc. He gives an example that shows why some trainers arrive at the front of the pack: "As time goes on, athletes are getting bigger and stronger as a group, and the latest research shows that dynamic work is better for warming those bigger bodies up, such as sprint drills and calisthenics, rather than the old methods of yoga-like warm-ups involving holding stretches."

Because Minor didn't have a coach fresh out of college and wanted to compete at a high level in his track career, he developed research methods to ensure he was taking advantage of all the best tools, methods, and philosophies available, which also paid off when he created his personal training business. He told us that most competitive collegiate athletes will just ask a coach what to do rather than do any research of their own, even if they're low on funds. A personal trainer with a monthly automatic withdrawal payment plan focusing on this market might capitalize on this large gap that needs to be filled.

Designing Your Business

Some entrepreneurs would rather walk on hot coals than sit down and write a business plan. Other would-be business owners get so caught up in planning every detail that they never get their businesses off the ground. You need to find a happy medium between these two extremes.

Your personal training company should start with a written business plan. Writing your plan down forces you to think it through and gives you a chance to examine it for consistency and thoroughness. Whether you've got years of personal training experience behind you or you're brand-new to the industry, you need a plan for your business.

This chapter will focus on a few issues particular to planning personal training businesses, but they are by no means all you need to consider when writing your plan.

If you're excited about your business, creating a business plan should be an exciting process. It will help you define and evaluate the overall feasibility of your concept, clarify your goals, and determine what you'll need for startup and long-term operations.

This is a living, breathing document that will provide you with a road map for your company. You'll use it as a guide, referring to it regularly as you work through the startup process and during the ongoing operation of your business. If you're going to be seeking outside financing, either in the form of loans or investors, your business plan will be the tool that convinces funding sources of your venture's worth.

Putting together a business plan is not a linear process, although the final product may look that way. As you work through it, you'll likely find yourself jumping from equipment requirements to cash flow forecasts to staffing, then back to cash flow, on to marketing, and back to equipment requirements. Take your time developing your plan. Whether you want to start a part-time business as a trainer going to clients' homes or establish a fully equipped studio, you're making a serious commitment, and you shouldn't rush into it.

Business Plan Elements

Though the specific content of your business plan will be unique, there is a basic format that you should follow. This will ensure that you address all the issues you need to, as well as provide lenders and investors with a document to evaluate that is organized in a familiar way. The basic elements are:

- *Front matter*. This includes your cover page, a table of contents, and a statement of purpose.
- *Business description*. Describe the specific personal training business you intend to start and list the reasons you can make it successful. This section should also include your business philosophy, goals, industry analysis, operations, inventory, and startup timetable.

- *Marketing plan.* Include an overview of the market, a description of your potential customers, a discussion of the advantages and drawbacks of your location, an analysis of the competition, and how you plan to promote your specific business.

- *Company organization.* Describe your management structure, your staffing needs and how you expect to meet them, the consultants and advisors who will be assisting you, your legal structure, and the certifications, licenses, permits, and other regulatory issues that will affect your operations.

- *Financial data.* This is where you show the source(s) of your startup capital and how you're going to use the money. Include information on real estate, fixtures, equipment, and insurance. You'll also include your financial statements: balance sheet, profit-and-loss statement, break-even analysis, personal financial statements, and personal federal income tax returns.

- *Financial projections.* Take your financial data and project it out to show what your business will do. Include projected income statements for three to five years, cash flow statements for three to five years, along with worst-case scenario income and cash flow statements to show what you'll do if your plan doesn't work. Keep in mind that if you're opening a studio, it typically will take until your second year to turn a profit. Realistically, when you take into account paying back your investors, it may take until the third year before you have positive cash flow, says Steve Tharrett, president of Club Industry Consulting, a Dallas-based fitness and sports industry consulting company. "Some type of negative cash flow is going to occur at the beginning," he says. "It's really rare that you'll ever make a profit your first year."

- *Summary.* Bring your plan together in this section. If you're trying to appeal to a funding source, use this section to reiterate the merits of your plan.

- *Appendices.* Use this for supporting documents, such as your facility design and layout, marketing studies, sample advertising, copies of leases, and licensing information.

Diana Broschka spent four months in 2007 writing a comprehensive business plan after her personal trainer, Phil Martens, and she decided to join forces to create 501FIT. They approached banks with the plan hoping to obtain SBA funding and were granted $300,000, but needed $350,000. Broschka was dead-on with the plan's projections and when the $50,000 difference began to affect progress, she contributed her personal savings to the business.

Martens and Broschka have developed a solid relationship with their bank and say it benefited them immensely. "In each of the three startup years we have been able to negotiate reprieves on our loan payments, thereby paying interest only during our

Bright Idea

Your business plan should include worst-case scenarios, both for your own benefit and for your funding sources. You'll benefit from thinking ahead about what you'll do if things don't go the way you want them to. You'll also increase the comfort level of your lenders/investors by demonstrating your ability to deal with adversity and potentially negative situations.

slow periods of summer," Broschka says. She elaborates on creating allies, "This has served us well and allowed us to keep the business moving forward. Our business took an unexpected hit between 2008 and 2009 when we had to sustain a 16 percent rent, tax, and operating expense increase. While this darn near put us out of business, we worked through it, stayed the course, and dug deeper to grow our client base."

Broschka encourages entrepreneurs to talk openly with debtors, exploring creative options and alternate payment plans. "Our landlord has worked through this challenge with us, and fortunately, due to honest, open, and very proactive conversation, he has even helped us with marketing and advertising expense supplements. Bottom line, in 2011 we finally satisfied the initial term of our lease and stabilized our rent expense," Broschka concludes.

To Market, to Market

Market research provides businesses with data that allows them to identify and reach particular market segments, and to solve or avoid marketing problems. A thorough market survey forms the foundation of any successful business. It would be impossible to develop marketing strategies or an effective product line without market research.

The goal of market research is for you to identify your market, find out where it is, and develop a strategy to communicate with prospective customers in a way that will convince them to buy from you. Market research will also give you information you need about your competitors. It's important for you to know what they're doing and how that meets—or doesn't meet—the needs of the market.

Marketing consultant Debbie LaChusa, of 10stepmarketing in Santee, California,

Smart Tip

Tip...

When you think your plan is complete, look at it with a fresh eye. Is it realistic? Does it take into account all the possible variables that could affect your operation? After you're satisfied, ask two or three professional associates you trust to evaluate your plan. Use their input to correct any problems before you invest time and money.

suggests checking with the major certifying organizations such as the American Council on Exercise (ACE) or the American College of Sports Medicine (ACSM) to find out how many certified trainers they have in your area. "This will give you an idea of the competition," she says. "Also ask if these organizations can provide any information about the specialties these trainers have, such as older adult fitness."

You'll also want to find out how many gyms, health clubs, and exercise studios are in your geographic service area. This speaks to both competition and opportunity. A simple browse through the Yellow Pages will tell you what you need to know. "Talk to some of the clubs and trainers to gauge how business is," LaChusa advises. "Is it weak? Strong? More than they can handle?"

Study the demographics. "Historically, data has shown that only about 20 percent of the population exercises [regularly]," says LaChusa. "Research the population of

> ### Bright Idea
> Update your business plan every year. Choose an annual date when you sit down with your plan, compare how closely your actual operation and results mirrored your forecasts, and decide if your plans for the coming year need adjusting. You will also need to make your financial forecasts for the coming year based on current and expected market conditions.

Smart Body, Smart Mind

A 2009 study reported in *Science Daily* conducted by the Sahlgrenska Academy and Sahlgrenska University Hospital reveals young adults who are fit have higher IQs and are more likely to go on to pursue higher education.

The study shows a clear link between good physical fitness and higher IQ test scores with the strongest influence in the areas of logical thinking and verbal comprehension. Fitness, rather than strength, was the indicator of higher test results. "Being fit means that you also have good heart and lung capacity and that your brain gets plenty of oxygen," says Michael Nilsson, professor at the Sahlgrenska Academy and chief physician at the Sahlgrenska University Hospital. "This may be one of the reasons why we can see a clear link with fitness, but not with muscular strength. We are also seeing that there are growth factors that are important."

The results also indicated that the men who were fit at age 18 were more likely later in life to pursue higher education and secure more qualified jobs.

adults between the ages of 18 and approximately 50 in your area. See if the math makes sense." You can get demographic information from the U.S. Census Bureau (see Appendix for contact information) or contact local government agencies for help.

One of the most basic elements of effective marketing is differentiating your business from the competition. One marketing consultant calls it "eliminating the competition." If you set yourself apart because no one else does exactly what you do, then you essentially have no competition. (In Chapter 7, you'll find more on ways to distinguish your business through serving a niche market.)

However, before you can differentiate yourself, you first need to understand who your competitors are and why your customers might patronize them. With the popularity of the internet, more and more of your competitors will have websites, which you can visit to find out what type of services they offer. Research what they do, how they operate, and how much they charge.

Of course, offering something no one else is offering could give you an edge in the market—but it could also mean that someone else has tried that and it didn't work. Don't make hasty decisions. Do your homework before finalizing your services.

The Competitor You Can't See

In most fields, competitors are fairly easy to identify. They are individuals or companies offering the same or a similar product or service to the market you're targeting. Of course, other personal trainers are your competitors. You might even consider some gyms and health clubs competition. But what might arguably be your biggest competitor is an intangible: the quick-fix attitude. People are besieged by advertisements, infomercials, and sales pitches that promise a physical transformation with little or no effort. Take these pills, and your fat will melt away. Spend just five minutes per day using this machine, and in two weeks you'll have washboard abs. Follow this diet, and you'll lose 30 pounds in 30 days.

Of course, these products and programs don't work and may even cause physical harm to the people who use them. After trying one gimmick after another without success, many people come to believe that they cannot change and are destined to be forever overweight and unfit.

Committed Long Term

Lifelong athletes understand that the day-to-day, average performance you accrue, as well as your normal nutritional habits, rather than the blips of frenzied inspiration of yo-yo dieting and crash exercising, determine what your body looks and feels like.

That expert consensus allows fit, healthy people to occasionally indulge in decadent foods and lounging without guilt or worry. How you behave 95 percent of the time determines your physique, not the remaining five. The urge to take the easy way out hits everyone, but patience and persistence always achieve more lasting, solid results in fitness.

Tyrone Minor's experience pulling a hamstring in college taught him how to focus on other things to stay fit during times of injury. "It's one thing to be an everyday person and have a setback," he says, "but another thing when you're competing, because your window of recovery is so small and you know the competitors around you are continuing to work. When you start to get healthier you have to be smart and not rush or you'll re-aggravate the injury." Tyrone admits that because of this experience he has a problem with the frenzy of trainers or ads emphasizing a promise to get fit in 30 to 60 days. He teaches his clients that fit is a lifestyle you can't change overnight. For example, for a 45-year-old woman to lose weight he typically tells her to set many small goals that work toward one larger, ultimate goal in the future. This way there is measurable progress made toward a long-term commitment, which is growing a new lifestyle with strong, deep roots.

Gunnar Peterson believes that plain old hard work, discipline, and healthy habits are all a body needs to be strong and fit, no matter what age you are. "I have a client who has done a fair share of performance-enhancing drugs who says I'm crazy not to do them, but I don't think I need to if I stick to my program. I can account for even a 4-pound difference in my weight by tweaking something in my workout or diet. I'm older than a lot of the people I train, but never miss a workout."

It's a challenging paradox. People know from experience that the quick fixes don't work, but rather than see the fault with that particular approach, they see it with themselves. After all, they reason, it worked for the people in the ads, so if it isn't working for them it must be their fault.

Messages pushing instant gratification for just about everything are virtually everywhere. As a personal trainer, you will be competing every day with the quick-fix gimmicks that don't work and have sabotaged people into believing they can look and feel great in a short time if they can just find the right product to use. You'll have to use logic and reason to persuade them to take a longer-term and healthier approach.

Minor believes many women who hire personal trainers are striving for a body that is not realistic because of the ultra thin women who are portrayed in the media all

Bright Idea

Don't just take a "me, too" approach to training. Develop your own professional personality, your own techniques, and your own program. Do things that will make you stand out from other personal trainers in a positive way.

around us. He frequently talks to his female clients about what size a healthy woman actually is to make sure they are focusing on the right goals to keep them on track.

Minor is always preaching to his clients about health and being the best person they can be, rather than comparing themselves with others, which, as he says, "prevents them from enjoying their own successes." An extremely fit and lean client of Minor's one day made the remark that he felt fit until he stood next to Minor. Minor then talked to him about how he himself had a very uncommon physique from competing into his 30s with intense training. The man had diminished his own accomplishments when he compared himself to someone else. All of that hard work, down the drain!

The Industry's Showcase

The more you know about the health and fitness industry in general, as well as personal training in particular, the easier it will be to develop an effective business plan.

An excellent source of information about the industry comes from conventions and trade shows. They're tremendous opportunities for education and networking. They're also an opportunity for industry leaders to showcase their products and services.

Two of the leading show coordinators are Club Industry and International Health, Racquet, and Sportsclub Association (IHRSA). Contact information is in the Appendix. Check out their show schedules and invest in attending, even if it means traveling to do so.

Selling Related Products

Some personal trainers limit their business to training; others take advantage of additional revenue opportunities such as nutritional supplements, exercise equipment, and clothing. Of course, if you have a studio, a refreshment area where you sell bottled water, smoothies, other beverages, and healthy snacks makes sense.

> **Tip...**
>
> ## Smart Tip
> Know someone who might be interested in investing in your business? Don't ask them for money right away. Tell them you're working on a business plan, and before you present it to an investor, you'd appreciate it if they could read it and give you some input. At best, they'll like the plan and offer to invest before you ask. At worst, you'll get some valuable input, and they'll let you know they don't want to invest before you have to risk rejection.

There are pros and cons to each approach. "I don't sell any products," says Jennifer B., the personal trainer in Brooklyn. "When people make a commitment to exercise, I'm very careful about adding on to their commitment or asking them to do something further that may be too much for them." On the other hand, these extra income sources can contribute handsomely to your overall profitability and keep you going during periodic slumps. Be careful that any sideline products or services don't detract from your primary business.

Establishing Policies and Procedures

Many aspects of your business will evolve and change as you get established and find out what works best for you and your clientele. But there are certain policies you should put in place from the very start. This protects both you and your clients from any problems or conflicts due to misunderstandings. These policies don't have to be complicated—in fact, the simpler and clearer, the better.

Cancellation Policy

Your most valuable commodity is your time, and it's something you can't replace or recover. If a client cancels at the last minute and doesn't pay you, that revenue opportunity is lost forever. A cancellation policy can protect you to some degree, but you must balance it against clients being upset at being forced to pay for something they didn't receive.

Jennifer B. says she started with a very strict policy requiring 24 hours' notice for cancellations, but she has become more flexible. "Obviously, things come up," she says. She tries to reschedule when possible, but reserves the right to charge for sessions missed at the last minute. Trainer Lynne W. of New York City takes a similar approach; she tries to reschedule, but if she can't, she charges for sessions cancelled with less than 24 hours' notice.

Facility owner Bill S. has a cancellation line that clients are supposed to call if they can't make their session, and the line forwards to his cell phone after hours. "If it's right before a training session, we ask clients to call their trainer, as well as the cancellation line, especially if it's an early morning client."

Beware!
Be consistent with your pricing and policies. You don't want two clients talking to each other at a party and finding out that they're paying different amounts for the same service, or that you're applying your policies differently.

Top 20 Forecasted Trends for 2012

The top 20 fitness trends, as identified by *ACSM* (American College of Sports Medicine) *Health and Fitness Journal's* "Worldwide Survey of Fitness Trends for 2012" are:

1. Educated, certified, and experienced fitness professionals
2. Strength training
3. Fitness programs for older adults
4. Exercise and weight loss
5. Children and obesity
6. Personal training
7. Core training
8. Group personal training
9. Zumba and other dance workouts*
10. Functional fitness
11. Yoga
12. Comprehensive health programming at the worksite
13. Boot camp
13. Outdoor activities*
14. Reaching new markets
16. Spinning (indoor cycling)
17. Sport specific training
18. Worker incentive programs
19. Wellness coaching
20. Physician referrals

*Indicates a top-20 position new for 2012

The author of this survey, Walter R. Thompson, Ph.D., FACSM, is a regents professor of Exercise Science in the Department of Kinesiology and Health (College of Education) at Georgia State University, where he has a second academic appointment in the Division of Nutrition (Byrdine F. Lewis School of Nursing and Health Professions).

Gunnar Peterson says he doesn't give any one of his clients priority over the others. "Celebrities' schedules tend to get pulled in many different directions but I can't blow one client's slot off for another's immediacy. Sure, I ask people occasionally if they can flex to help coordinate scheduling challenges, but I do that across the board and treat everyone equally."

Late Policy

There are two sides to a late policy: when the client is late and when the trainer is late.

If a client is running late, your policy could be that they don't get to make up their time. But if the client has a good reason and is not habitually late, and there is room in the schedule without inconveniencing another client, you could allow some extra minutes at the end of the session. If you have trainers working for you, you'll likely want to take a harder line with their tardiness. If a trainer is more than five minutes late, for example, the session could be complimentary to the client, but the trainer would have to reimburse the business what the client would have paid.

Jennifer B. says when she or one of her trainers is late, they make up the time either in that session or in another. Lynne W. says if the client is late, the session still ends on time. If she is late, she tries to get the time in at that session or a later one, or she'll adjust the fee.

Dealing with a Difficult Client

A chronically late client is a sign you've got a difficult client. Other symptoms include not paying for training on time, constantly complaining that they're not getting results (even though they're not following your professional advice), and not being motivated to push themselves hard enough, says New York trainer Mike Hood. To help deal with such a client, it's important to keep things on a professional level, he says. "By always keeping the professional tone, rather than the 'friend tone,' this allows you to maintain control of the situation," he explains. "And establish at the onset that you take what you do seriously, that you are a professional and you care. Lay down the ground rules for cancellations and set the standard from day one on things like lateness, payment, and what they are responsible for in your relationship in order to achieve the results they're looking for."

▲

"Clients respect a trainer who stays on schedule," says trainer Richard Cotton. "The trainer keeps clients longer, and that's reflected in the income."

Be sure to communicate your cancellation and late policies clearly during your initial consultation so that clients aren't surprised or upset when you enforce them. Insist that your clients respect your time, and make it mutual. Cotton likens it to doctor's appointments: "Doctors are so busy that we make sure we make it to our appointments because it may be a couple of months before we can get another one," he says. "That same kind of feeling should exist with the trainer."

Think About the Unthinkable

The idea that one of your clients may become ill or injured during a session is not a pleasant one, but it's one you need to think about. You and all the trainers on your staff should be CPR and first-aid certified.

CPR courses train people to recognize and care for breathing and cardiac emergencies. To maintain your CPR certification, you must take a refresher course annually. First-aid certification courses will teach you how to deal with bone, joint, and muscle injuries, heat-related injuries, bleeding, and how to move victims.

Beyond being able to provide immediate first aid, you need a total emergency response plan. This plan will serve as your guide for any situation where a person is injured or lives are in danger, from a minor sprain to a major fire. Dialing 911 is not a one-size-fits-all answer.

Your emergency response plan should be basic—sufficient enough to provide the structure that will reduce further injury and save lives, simple enough that it can be remembered and properly carried out. See the sample emergency procedure policy on page 29. You should think through all the possible emergency situations you might conceivably encounter. The idea is to prepare for the unexpected—keeping in mind that there is no way you can predict what is going to happen.

Consider these possible scenarios:

- A client drops a weight on his foot, possibly breaking a bone.
- A client complains of chest pain and shortness of breath while exercising.
- While working with a client in a gym, an electrical short causes a fire in the cardiovascular equipment area.
- While working with a client in your studio, a disgruntled former boyfriend comes in and begins threatening you both.

- While working with a client in her home, her preteen son is playing in another room and manages to sustain a serious cut or injury.

Some of these scenarios may sound far-fetched, but they are common occurrences that could easily happen while you are present. It's important that you think about what you'll do in those circumstances. Have an emergency procedure policy written down so your employees know exactly what to do. This not only educates them, it also protects you from a liability perspective.

Sample Emergency Procedure Policy

WE MOVE YOU
Personal Trainers

Our goal is to provide a safe, comfortable environment for our clients and to design programs that can be implemented without injury. However, we recognize that there may be times when an emergency situation occurs and outside assistance is required. In those cases, we will administer appropriate immediate first aid and/or CPR. If the victim is unconscious, we will check his/her breathing and pulse; then we will follow these procedures:

1. Dial 911. (If two or more staff members are present, one should be sent to call for emergency assistance and the other(s) should stay with the victim to provide what care is possible.)

2. Be prepared to provide the emergency dispatcher with the exact location, the telephone number from which the call is being made, the name of the caller, a description of what happened, the number of people involved, the condition of the victim(s) (i.e., alert, unconscious, etc.), and a description of what assistance or first aid has been rendered.

3. Follow whatever instructions the dispatcher gives you. In many situations, the dispatcher will be able to tell you how to best care for the victim.

4. Do not hang up until the dispatcher tells you to.

5. Once the dispatcher tells you to hang up, return to the victim.

Whenever something happens, begin with an assessment of the situation. How serious is the injury? Is the injured person able to aid himself? Is there immediate danger to others at the location (for example, in the case of a fire)?

Once you've assessed the situation, take the appropriate steps. That might mean administering first aid or CPR. It could mean calling the police, fire department, or emergency medical personnel. If you have a commercial location, be sure your telephone number, address, and directions to your location from the nearest emergency service facility are posted by each telephone. Don't expect anyone to remember these details in a crisis.

> **Tip...**
>
> ### Smart Tip
>
> CPR classes as well as courses in first-aid basics and emergency response techniques are available through your local chapter of the American Red Cross, your local fire department, and area hospitals. You and all your employees should hold these certifications.

When the situation is under control, complete an incident report for your files (see page 34 for a report you can copy and use in your business). Be sure to get the names and contact information of everyone who witnessed the incident; this will be critical if litigation should arise. Describe the incident completely, including details such as exactly what the client was doing at the time (exercising, resting in the locker room, entering or exiting the facility, etc.) and what the trainer was doing at the time. Include a description of the procedures you took and the results. For example, if you administered first aid and the client declined further assistance, note that. If you administered CPR, called for emergency medical services, and the client was taken to the hospital by ambulance, record that for your files.

Are You Liable?

In our intensely litigious society, no business owner can afford to ignore liability issues. In Chapter 10, we'll discuss release forms and liability waivers, but it's important to know that these documents alone will not prevent you from becoming the defendant in a lawsuit.

What is the extent of your liability if a client is injured while under your supervision? Your defense will depend on a number of issues, including whether you are adequately trained and certified for the activity involved; the adequacy of your pre-program screening and testing; whether or not the client signed an informed consent, release and assumption of the risk consent form; and whether or not your instructions and advice were within acceptable ranges based on the client's physical condition and circumstances.

Another area of risk is that of nutrition and supplement counseling. "It's important to not go out of your scope of practice," says Tony Ordas, former director of certification for the American Council on Exercise (ACE). "One challenge we've had is educating people that [if] they aren't registered dietitians, they shouldn't be recommending, supplying, and prescribing nutritional supplements."

Many personal trainers are very knowledgeable on these issues through their own personal interest and study, and it's common for clients to turn to their trainers for guidance on diet and supplements. One of the key concerns in these situations is the unauthorized practice of medicine or other licensed healthcare disciplines. Unless you are well-trained and certified, this can be dangerous territory. A lawsuit on record explains why: When a 37-year-old woman died after following her trainer's advice on consuming nutritional and weight-loss products, her family sued the trainer, the club where the trainer worked, the store where the supplements were purchased, and the manufacturers of the supplements.

The suit alleged that one of the five substances the trainer recommended contained ephedrine. The woman was also taking hypertension medication prescribed by her physician, and these substances should not be taken at the same time. The suit claimed that the woman told her trainer about the medication she was taking. She suffered a stroke while exercising and died a few hours later. The trainer learned a very painful and tragic lesson.

Educating your clients on knowing how hard to push themselves could influence decisions you'll make on how much liability insurance to purchase. Tyrone Minor says that once you become a certified trainer you can work with your certification company to determine how much insurance you'll need.

"It's hard to make that decision for someone else," says Minor. "Even the most well-intentioned trainer could injure someone and it could just be a freak accident and not the cause of anything the trainer may have done wrong."

Minor advises trainers to educate their clients about what is trivial irritation and what may be more serious signals. "Sometimes clients feel tightness in their bodies and don't communicate it to you because they are too busy wanting to please you—to work hard for you. You may be making decisions based on a different perception of how they are feeling. Had you known they felt this tightness, you wouldn't have had them perform in the same way. That's one way

Beware!

Ignore a small problem and it can quickly turn into a major one. If any sort of incident occurs where you have potential liability or if anyone (client or not) threatens to sue you for any reason, notify your insurance company immediately and let them help you through the process.

injuries can occur. Even though clients don't want to let you down, you can teach them the difference between a red flag and simple soreness."

Are You on a Mission?

When you're serious about a business, you work hard to develop a mission—that is, you figure out what you're doing, how and where it's being done, and who your customers are. Problems can arise, however, when that mission is not clearly articulated into a statement, written down, and communicated to others. We've provided a worksheet on page 35 to help you get started.

"A mission statement defines what an organization is, why it exists, its reason for being," says Gerald Graham, R.P. Clinton Distinguished Professor of Management and immediate past dean of the W. Frank Barton School of Business at Wichita State University. "Writing it down and communicating it to others creates a sense of commonality and a more coherent approach to what you're trying to do."

Even in a very small company, a written mission statement helps everyone involved see the big picture and keeps them focused on the true goals of the business. According to Graham, at a minimum your mission statement should define who your primary customers are, the products and services you produce, and the geographical location in which you operate.

501FIT's mission, prominently placed on its website, is "At 501F1T we take pride in providing our clients a clean, safe and fun spirited fitness environment. We welcome everyone with any fitness experience, goal or need. We promote confidence and unsurpassed results in a friendly way. Our group strength and cardio fitness class programs create accountability with a positive and goal oriented approach. Our clients (YOU) are #1. Call or visit us today and find out for yourself how 501F1T is the premier mid-sized fitness option for you in the Twin Cities."

Jennifer Brilliant says her mission statement is: "To guide others toward the amazing experience of living in their bodies with confidence and joy." Another trainer we interviewed had a mission statement that reads: "We are caregivers. We try not only to physically inspire others, but also to give people the faith to ask more of themselves. It is our mission to promote healthy lifestyle changes in a positive manner until all of our clients' dreams come true."

A mission statement should be short—usually just one to three sentences. A good idea is to cap it at 100 words. Anything longer isn't a mission statement and will probably be confusing.

Once you have articulated your message, communicate it as often as possible to everyone in the company, along with clients and suppliers. "Post it on the wall, hold meetings to talk about it, and include a reminder of the statement in employee correspondence," says Graham.

Graham explains that it is more important to adequately communicate the mission statement to employees than to customers. "Sometimes an organization will try to use a mission statement primarily for promotion and, as an aside, use it to help employees identify what business they're in," he says. "That doesn't work very well. The most effective mission statements are developed strictly for internal communication and discussion, and then if something promotional comes out of it, fine." In other words, your mission statement doesn't have to be clever or catchy—just accurate.

Though your mission statement may never win an advertising or creativity award, it can still be a very effective customer relations tool. One idea is to print your mission statement on a page, have every employee sign it, and provide every prospective and new customer with a copy. You can even include it on your brochures and invoices.

Finally, make sure your suppliers know what your mission statement is. It will help them serve you better if they understand what you're all about.

▲

Injury or Emergency Incident Report

Date: _____ Time of incident: _____ A.M./P.M.

Name of injured person: _____

Address: _____

Phone: _____

Manager/trainer on duty: _____

Location of incident: _____

Note if it occurred in the client's home or office, at a gym, or your own studio, which-ever is applicable.

Equipment involved: _____

Description of incident: _____

_____

_____

_____

_____

Emergency procedures taken by staff:

○ First aid   ○ CPR   ○ Emergency services [police/fire/medical]

Description of emergency procedures and results: _____

_____

_____

_____

Witnesses:

Name: _____

Phone: _____

Name: _____

Phone: _____

Name: _____

Phone: _____

Mission Statement Worksheet

To develop an effective mission statement, answer these questions:

1. What products and/or services do we produce? _____

    _____

    _____

2. What geographical location do we operate in? _____

    _____

    _____

3. Why does our company exist? Whom do we serve? What is our purpose?

    _____

    _____

4. What are our strengths, weaknesses, opportunities, and threats? _____

    _____

    _____

5. Considering the above, along with our expertise and resources, what business should we be in? _____

    _____

    _____

6. What is important to us? What do we stand for? _____

    _____

    _____

Structuring Your Business

Building a business is much like building a house: You need a foundation, frame, and roof, and then you can put up the walls and worry about details like furnishings. Let's take a look at what you need for the foundation, frame, and roof of your company.

▲

Legal Structure

One of the first decisions you'll need to make about your new business is the legal structure of your company. This is an important decision. It can affect your financial liability; the amount of taxes you pay; the degree of ultimate control you have over the company; as well as your ability to raise money, attract investors, and ultimately sell your business. However, legal structure shouldn't be confused with operating structure. Attorney Robert S. Bernstein, of Bernstein Law Firm in Pittsburgh, explains the difference: "The legal structure is the ownership structure—who actually owns the company. The operating structure defines who makes management decisions and runs the company."

A sole proprietorship is owned by the proprietor, a partnership is owned by the partners, and a corporation is owned by the shareholders. Another business structure is the limited liability company (LLC), which combines the tax advantages of a sole proprietorship with the liability protection of a corporation. The rules on LLCs vary by state; check with your state's department of corporations for the latest requirements.

Sole proprietorships and partnerships generally can be operated however the owners choose. In a corporation, the shareholders typically elect directors, who in turn elect officers, who then employ other people to run and work in the company. But it's entirely possible for a corporation to have only one shareholder and to essentially function as a sole proprietorship. In any case, how you plan to operate the company should not be a major factor in your choice of legal structures.

So what goes into choosing a legal structure? The first point, says Bernstein, is who is actually making the decision on the legal structure. If you're starting the company by yourself, you don't need to take anyone else's preferences into consideration. "But if there are multiple people involved, you need to consider how you're going to relate to each other in the business," he says. "You also need to consider the issue of asset protection and limiting your liability in the event things don't go well."

Something else to think about is your target customer and what their perception will be of your structure. While it's not necessarily true, Bernstein says, "There is a tendency to believe that the legal form of a business has some relationship to the sophistication of the owners, with the sole proprietor as the least sophisticated and the corporation as the most sophisticated." It might enhance your image if you incorporate, especially if your goal is to contract to health clubs or work with health-care providers or big companies.

Your image notwithstanding, the biggest advantage of forming a corporation is in the area of asset protection, which, says Bernstein, is the process of making sure that the assets that you don't want to put into the business don't stand liable for the

---

Physical Inactivity and Diabetes

With data from a 2008 diabetes and inactivity study the Centers for Disease Control found which states' residents are the most and least physically active.

The regions with the highest rates of leisure-time physical inactivity are the South and Appalachia, which also have high rates of diagnosed diabetes and obesity. Specific states within the region where residents are least likely to use their free time for physical activities are Alabama, Kentucky, Louisiana, Mississippi, Oklahoma, and Tennessee.

Conversely, areas with the most active residents during their free time are the West Coast, Colorado, Minnesota, and parts of the Northeast.

---

business's debt. However, to take advantage of the protection a corporation offers, you must respect the corporation's identity. That means maintaining the corporation as a separate entity, keeping your corporate and personal funds separate (even if you are the sole shareholder), and following your state's rules regarding holding annual meetings and other record-keeping requirements.

Is any one of these structures better than another? No. We found personal trainers operating as sole proprietors, partners, and corporations, and they made their choices based on what was best for their particular situation, which is what you should do.

Jennifer Brilliant, the personal trainer in Brooklyn, says she formed an LLC after operating for many years as a sole proprietor because she felt it was less risky and more professional.

Do you need an attorney to set up a corporation or a partnership? Bernstein says there are plenty of good do-it-yourself books and kits on the market, and most of the state agencies that oversee corporations have guidelines you can use. Even so, it's always a good idea to have a lawyer at least look over your documents before you file them, just to make sure they are complete and will allow you to truly function as you want to.

"Business partnership, in my opinion, is on the same complication level as marriage," Diana Broschka says. "While it is advantageous for business partners to bring in different perspectives and skill sets, that very paradigm is both a challenge and benefit at the same time. Phil [Martens] was a solo business owner and visionary for many years before we connected in partnership, and the transition for him to partnership was, I believe, more difficult than for me, as I come from 20-plus years of corporate experience and have a built-in system of accountabilities, report abilities, and collaboration."

Finally, remember that your choice of legal structure is not an irrevocable decision, although if you're going to make a switch, it's easier to go from the simpler forms to the more sophisticated ones than the other way around. Bernstein says the typical pattern is to start as a sole proprietor, and then move up to a corporation as the business grows. But if you need the asset protection of a corporation from the beginning, start out that way. "If you're going to the trouble to start a business, decide on a structure and put it all together," says Bernstein. It's worth the extra effort to make sure it's really going to work."

> ### Smart Tip
>
> Not all attorneys are created equal, and you may need more than one. For example, the lawyer who can best guide you in contract negotiations may not be the most effective counsel when it comes to employment issues. Ask about areas of expertise and specialization before retaining a lawyer. Find lawyers in your area who adhere to the Nolo pledge of high standards on www.nolo.com.

Business Insurance

It takes a lot to start a business—even a small one—so protect your investment with adequate insurance. If you're homebased, don't assume your homeowner's or renters' policy covers your business equipment; chances are it doesn't. If you're located in a commercial facility, be prepared for your landlord to require proof of certain levels of liability insurance when you sign the lease. In either case, you'll need coverage for your equipment, supplies, and other valuables.

A smart approach to insurance is to find an agent who works with other fitness-related businesses. The agent should be willing to help you analyze your needs, evaluate the risks you're willing to accept and the risks you need to insure against, and work with you to keep your insurance costs down.

You should also check with industry associations that offer professional liability coverage as part of their membership benefits. For example, Jennifer B. buys her professional liability coverage through an association. Richard C. says associations are probably the best source for professional liability coverage for personal trainers. Rates vary depending on the amount of coverage you want, as well as other factors, but typically you'll pay about $400 per year for professional liability insurance.

Typically, homebased businesses will want to make sure their equipment and supplies are covered against theft and damage by a covered peril (such as fire or flood) and that they have some liability protection if someone (either a customer or an employee) is injured on their property. If you decide to open a studio in a commercial location, your landlord will probably require certain levels of general liability coverage as part of the terms of your lease. Once your business

> **Smart Tip** Tip...
>
> When you purchase insurance on your equipment and inventory, ask what documentation the insurance company requires before you have to file a claim. That way, you'll be sure to maintain appropriate records, and the claims process will be easier if it is ever necessary.

is up and running, consider business interruption insurance to replace lost revenue and to cover related costs if you are ever unable to operate due to covered circumstances. Also, if you use your vehicle for business, be sure it is adequately covered.

Additionally, being a personal trainer is a physically demanding profession, so you should consider purchasing disability insurance in addition to health insurance—especially if you're operating a solo business and cannot rely on others to pick up the slack if you get injured or become ill. In general, disability insurance payments will be about 70 percent of your gross income. Short-term disability policies have a maximum benefit period of up to two years, while long-term disability policies feature benefit periods ranging from several years to full life.

It's best to purchase a "non-cancelable contract," which locks in benefits and rates, writes lawyer and business author Steven D. Strauss in *USA Today*. Avoid a "conditionally renewable" policy that permits the insurer to change benefits or rates. Also, look for a disability policy that defines your occupation specifically, called an "own-occupation disability" policy, Strauss advises.

> **Smart Tip** Tip...
>
> Sit down with your insurance agent once every year and review your insurance needs. As your company grows, they are sure to change. Also, insurance companies are always developing new products to meet the needs of the growing small-business market, and it's possible one of these new policies is appropriate for you.

The insurance industry is responding to the special needs of small businesses by developing affordable products that provide coverage on equipment, liability, and loss of income. In most cases, one of the new insurance products designed for homebased businesses will provide sufficient coverage.

Licenses and Permits

Most cities and counties require business operators to obtain various licenses and permits to comply with local regulations. While you are still in the planning stages, check with your local planning and zoning department or city/county business license department to find out what licenses and permits you will need and how to obtain them. You may need some or all of the following:

- *Occupational license or permit.* This is typically required by the city (or county if you are not within an incorporated city) for just about every business operating within its jurisdiction. License fees are essentially a tax, and the rates vary widely based on the location and type of business. As part of the application process, the licensing bureau will check to make sure there are no zoning restrictions prohibiting you from operating. This is particularly important if

Music to Their Ears

Many people like to work out to music. It helps them maintain their exercise rhythm and combats boredom. When you're working with clients in their own homes or offices and they want to play tapes or CDs they own, that's fine. But when you use music in a studio, a class, or any other setting that may be deemed a "public performance," you need a license.

Songwriters and music publishers own the rights to their music, and they have the right to grant or deny permission to use their property and to receive compensation for that use. They receive compensation by being members of performing-rights organizations that collect fees from users through licensing public performances of the works. Fees for fitness facilities vary by the size of the facility, the number of students, and the use of the music (background or instructional use).

The three major performing rights organizations in the United States are the American Society of Composers, Authors, and Publishers (ASCAP), Broadcast Music Inc. (BMI), and SESAC. Contact them for complete information on the procedures and costs involved in obtaining music licenses. (See the Appendix for contact information.)

Copying songs from different tapes or CDs for use in classes or with clients without paying music-licensing fees is a violation of U.S. copyright and trademark laws. So is duplicating for your colleagues a tape or CD purchased from a fitness music company. Just as you wouldn't want anyone to steal from you, don't steal songwriters' and music publishers' right to earn just compensation for their work.

you are homebased and clients will be coming to your home for their sessions.

- *Fire department permit.* If your business is open to the public, you may be required to have a permit from the local fire department.

- *Sign permit.* Many cities and suburbs have sign ordinances that restrict the size, location, and sometimes the lighting and type of sign you can use in front of your business. Landlords may also impose their own restrictions. Most residential areas forbid signs altogether. To avoid costly mistakes, check regulations and secure the written approval of your landlord before you invest in a sign.

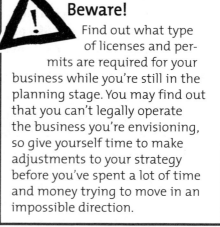

Beware!
Find out what type of licenses and permits are required for your business while you're still in the planning stage. You may find out that you can't legally operate the business you're envisioning, so give yourself time to make adjustments to your strategy before you've spent a lot of time and money trying to move in an impossible direction.

- *State license.* Many states require persons engaged in certain occupations to hold licenses or occupational permits. Often, these people must pass state examinations before they can conduct business. States commonly require licensing for auto mechanics, plumbers, electricians, building contractors, collection agents, insurance agents, real estate brokers, those involved in repossession, and personal service providers such as doctors, nurses, barbers, cosmetologists, etc. It is highly unlikely that you will need a state license to operate your personal training business, but it's a good idea to check with your state's occupation licensing entity to be sure.

Professional Advisors

As a business owner, you may be the boss, but you can't be expected to know everything. You'll occasionally need to turn to professionals for information and assistance. It's a good idea to establish relationships with these professionals before you get into a crisis situation.

To shop for a professional service provider, ask friends and associates for recommendations. You might also check with your local chamber of commerce or trade association for referrals. Find someone who understands your industry and specific business, and appears eager to work with you. Check them out with the Better Business Bureau and the appropriate state licensing agency before committing yourself.

▲

Many of the business owners we talked with have ongoing relationships with accountants and know of an attorney they can call on if they need one. They also have other advisors. As the owner of a personal training company, the professional service providers you're likely to need include:

- *Attorney.* You need a lawyer who practices in the area of business law and who is honest and appreciates your patronage. In most parts of the United States, there are many lawyers willing to compete for the privilege of serving you. Interview several and choose one you feel comfortable with. Be sure to clarify the fee schedule ahead of time and get your agreement in writing. Keep in mind that good commercial lawyers don't come cheap. If you want good advice, you must be willing to pay for it. Your attorney should review all contracts, leases, letters of intent, informed consent/release forms, waivers, and other legal documents before you sign or begin using them. He or she can also help you collect bad debts and establish personnel policies and procedures. Of course, if you are unsure of the legal ramifications of any situation, call your attorney immediately.

- *Accountant.* Among your outside advisors, your accountant is likely to have the greatest impact on the success or failure of your business. If you are forming a corporation, your accountant should counsel you on tax issues during startup. On an ongoing basis, your accountant can help you organize the statistical data concerning your business, assist in charting future actions based on past performance, and advise you on your overall financial strategy regarding purchasing, capital investment, and other matters related to your business goals. A good accountant will also serve as a tax advisor, making sure you are in compliance

Senior Fitness Research Findings

In a study conducted by the Department of Neuro and Locomotor Science at the Akita University School of Medicine in Japan, 80 postmenopausal women with osteoporosis were given simple low-intensity back-strengthening exercises to do at home for four months. The hypothesis was that this type of exercise not only improved the inner muscles of the back in the test subjects, but that it improved their quality of life and spinal range of motion, but also decreased their risk of vertebral fractures. Read more about this study at: www. pubmed.gov.

with all applicable regulations and that you don't overpay any taxes. You may want your accountant to hold a CPA (Certified Public Accountant) designation. CPAs are licensed, regulated, and insured; their rates will likely be higher than a noncertified accountant, but the enhanced level of service is worth it.

- *Insurance agent.* A good independent insurance agent can assist you with all aspects of your business insurance, from general liability to employee benefits. Look for an agent who works with a wide range of insurers and understands your particular business. This agent should be willing to explain the details of various types of coverage, consult with you to determine the most appropriate coverage, help you understand the degree of risk you are taking, work with you in developing risk-reduction programs, and assist in expediting any claims. Your agent should also understand if you choose to purchase particular types of coverage from someone else. For example, many personal trainers find that the professional liability coverage they need is less expensive when purchased through a professional association or a specialty insurance carrier.

- *Banker.* You need a business bank account and a relationship with a banker. Don't just choose the bank you've always done your personal banking with; it may not be the best bank for your business. Interview several bankers before making a decision on where to place your business. Once your account is opened, maintain a relationship with the banker. Periodically sit down and review your accounts and the services you use to make sure you are getting the package most appropriate for your situation. Ask for advice if you have financial questions or problems. When you need a loan or a bank reference to provide to creditors, the relationship you've established will work in your favor.

- *Consultants.* The consulting industry is booming, and for good reason. Consultants can provide valuable, objective input on all aspects of your business. Consider hiring a business consultant to evaluate your business plan, or a marketing consultant to assist you in that area. When you are ready to hire employees, a human resources consultant may help you avoid some costly mistakes. Consulting fees vary widely, depending on the individual's experience, location, and field of expertise. If you can't afford to hire a consultant, consider contacting the business school at the nearest college or university and hiring an MBA student to help you.

- *Computer expert.* You'll use a computer to manage your business and track client information. Your computer and data are extremely valuable assets; so if you don't know much about computers, find someone to help you select a system and the appropriate software. Make sure they'll be available to help you maintain, troubleshoot, and expand your system as you need it.

What's In a Name?

Your company name can be an important marketing tool. A well-chosen name can work very hard for you; an ineffective name means you have to work much harder at marketing your firm and letting people know what you have to offer.

Regardless of what type of business you're in, your company name should clearly identify what you do in a way that will appeal to your target market. For example, Richard Cotton says if you want to a attract bodybuilding clientele, choose a name along the lines of "Muscle Madness Personal Training." If you're going for baby boomers having trouble getting started with a program, choose something less intimidating. In any case, the name should be short, catchy, and memorable. It should also be easy to pronounce and spell—people who can't say your company name may use you, but they'll be less likely to refer you to anyone else.

Tyrone Minor has strangers approach him out of curiosity and admiration because of his physique, such as the time when a man walked up to him at the beach and asked about his workout program. Though Minor is quite modest, he did tell us that he was

501F1T gym

shirtless at the time, and because of the repetitive use of the word "chiseled" people use to describe him, he decided to name his business Chizel Inc.

501F1T, straight and to the point, is the address people go to for fitness.

Gunnar Peterson's name is passed by referral often and remains the name of his business to date. Organic Stretching™ describes the art of healing Pat Henry developed and reaches out to those seeking such. Many personal trainers simply use their own name and the primary service they provide. One entrepreneur we interviewed simply put her name in front of "Yoga and Personal Training, LLC." "That's what it is," she says. "Just to be straightforward made sense to me."

If you want to get creative, brainstorm as many names you can think of and ask a friend to help. Don't worry about how they sound—just come up with a possible list, and evaluate it later. As you create, think about the mission statement of your business and the message you would like to convey to potential customers so that they're inspired and intrigued enough to check out your services.

An alternative approach is to use some sort of regional or other descriptive designation, plus the primary service category offered. This helps search engines and possible customers find you online because these are the terms they search with for services like yours. Yet another possibility is that you may decide your business doesn't need a name other than your own. We have provided a worksheet to help you brainstorm your company name on page 49.

The Name Game

Use a systematic approach when naming your company. Once you've decided on two or three possibilities, take the following steps.

❍ *Check the name for effectiveness and functionality.* Does it quickly and easily convey what you do? Is it easy to say and spell? Is it memorable in a positive way? Ask several of your friends and associates to serve as a focus group to help you evaluate the name's impact.

❍ *Search for potential conflicts in your local market.* Find out if any other local or regional business serving your market area has a name so similar that yours might confuse the public.

❍ *Check for legal availability.* Exactly how you do this depends on the legal structure you choose. Typically, sole proprietorships and partnerships

▲

The Name Game, continued

operating under a name other than that of the owner(s) are required by the county, city, or state to register their fictitious name. Even if it's not required, it's a good idea because that means no one else can use that name. Corporations usually operate under their corporate name. In either case, you need to check with the appropriate regulatory agency to be sure the name you choose is available. Check out Nolo's business naming and trademark registration advice to cover all bases at www.nolo.com.

○ *Search your possible name variations online.* The easiest way to find out if a domain name is taken is to try it out and see what happens (a domain name is something like www.inshapetraining.com). You also can check this on hosting sites such as www.register.com or www.networksolutions.com. If someone else is already using your name as a domain, consider coming up with something else. Even if you have no intention of developing a website of your own, the use could be confusing to your customers.

○ *Check to see if the name conflicts with any name listed on your state's trademark register.* Your state department of commerce can either help you or direct you to the correct agency. Check the Thomas Register at thomasnet.com and the United States Patent and Trademark Office (PTO) at uspto.gov/main/trademarks.htm to search registered and unregistered trademarks.

○ *Register your business name.* Once the name you've chosen passes these tests, you need to protect it by registering it with the appropriate state agency; again, your state department of commerce can help you. Though most personal training businesses are local operations, many grow to a regional and even national scope. If you expect to be doing business on a national level, you should also register your name with the PTO.

A Word Is Worth a Thousand Pictures

If you need some help in your brainstorming process, go to www.thesaurus.com. Choose some fitness, physical, energy, and health-related words to plug into its search box. Then enter the words into two columns. Mix the words up so that catchy combinations appear. Try inserting your name or city name into the mix in a third column. Keep brainstorming with www.thesaurus.com and fill in the third column in this worksheet using the head start we created for you:

Fitness	Bloom	_____
Fine	Vigor	_____
Health	Chutzpah	_____
Energy	Force	_____
Spitfire	Speed	_____
Guts and	Gumption	_____
Trim	Perfection	_____
Robust	Overhaul	_____
Muscles and	Moxie	_____
Strength	Summit	_____
Anatomy	Peak	_____
Mighty	Physique	_____
Euphoric	Prime	_____
Steamroller	Stamina	_____
Brawny	Reaction	_____
Powerhouse	Steam	_____
Vital	Pizzaz	_____
Iron	Force	_____
Steel	Lightning	_____
Strapping	Speed	_____
Herculean	Feat	_____
Enduring	Velocity	_____
Force	Fervor	_____

Locating and Setting Up Your Business

There are several ways to keep your costs and risk factors down in the first few years of growing your business. Keeping your obligations simple while allowing yourself the greatest freedom to charge what you please, keep 100 percent of the profits, create your own policies, and develop your own style will ensure that as your reputation grows you are rewarded accordingly. There are benefits to being a gym contractor or employee, most of which fall under the category of being unencumbered when your shift is over: How much of your income is it worth to have someone else handle the responsibilities of insurance, booking, billing, paying the rent, and maintaining equipment and marketing?

Independence or Autonomy?

Too often trainers pair up with health clubs in hopes of growing a client base but become disillusioned with their cut of the profits and lack of freedom to try new things that don't fall under the clubs' policies. Pairing up with a health club can be a great learning experience in the beginning of your career, but make sure you have clear plans on when you'll fly off on your own and how you'll break free from that partnership.

Working independently part time in a different facility to build your client base while you work part time for someone else can help the problem some trainers face when they want to dissolve their club ties and keep their client following. Contractual obligations can prevent you from keeping the clients you met under the employ of a club, which is fair since they're paying for all of the extras that allow you to practice your craft.

If you are new to the industry a wise approach might be to start small, working with clients at their locations. Build a solid reputation and following first, then look at renting a commercial studio or low-cost alternative venue.

Become familiar with the various gyms and health clubs in your area. If you find a client who is already a member of a club, they may want you to work with them there. Or you may have clients who want to work with you in a gym setting and will look to you for advice as to which gym to join.

Whether you're starting from scratch as a solo enterprise or trying to build your client base part time, consider the following creative venue ideas.

Recreation and Community Centers

Tyrone Minor of Chizel Inc. finds unique situations like recreation centers, client homes, and parks to keep his costs down. Some cities offer low annual fees for recreation centers as a perk for their residents, such as the St. Paul, Minnesota Parks and Recreation Centers. For an annual $30 fee residents enjoy five workout gyms throughout the city filled with much of the same equipment featured at expensive health clubs. There is also swimming available for a small fee, should you decide to incorporate water aerobics, therapy, or lap swimming as part of your routine. Other cities have similar programs.

Home Gyms

You can custom outfit client homes to suit your teachings with a little crafty shopping, and your new outfitting service can become an additional source of income. Some clients will already have existing home gyms fully loaded but others may not even have considered the idea of a home gym and welcome the suggestion. You may find some clients happy and relieved to know you'll not only create a home gym for them but also keep their costs down by shopping for used equipment and training them in their homes, saving them time and commute costs.

When Lynne Wells first started as a personal trainer in New York City, she worked with clients in a gym and paid a fee to the gym for that privilege. Today, she works with clients primarily at their homes. If you're going to work from home, your space requirements are minimal and your startup costs can be as low as a few hundred dollars (depending on what office and exercise equipment you already own). You'll need a small area to do your administrative work and a place to store any equipment you might use. A clear space in your living room is all you need if you do training at home, or you may set up a dedicated workout room if you have the space.

Creating Custom Home Gyms for Profit

Tyrone Minor helps clients set up their own home gyms by first taking a detailed account of their goals and budgets. He then scours www.craigslist.org for used equipment in great condition and if when he inspects it finds it safe and functioning well, purchases it, cleans it up, makes repairs or upgrades to make it perfect, and then puts it into a home gym package for the customer priced at a markup he can profit from. This is a great deal for the customer because their custom shopper is also their trainer and understands their goals. Minor can help affect home workouts by setting up these gyms, therefore increasing the chances his clients will stay on track with their fitness goals.

Personal Training Studios and Private Gyms

Renting small personal training studios and privately owned gyms is another way to keep costs down, which Minor takes advantage of, using several around the city, each chosen so clients don't have to travel far to see him. Each has its own inventory of equipment. "Expect to pay $15 to $20 an hour for this kind of rental. Just Google search 'personal training studio' and the name of your city," Minor says.

Mobile Gym Units

Another location option is a mobile studio. Outfit a van or mobile home with exercise equipment so you can take a gym to your clients' homes or offices. Decide what type of equipment you'd like to have, then consult with a recreational vehicle dealer or a van conversion or customizing shop to find out how much it will cost you to get the setup you want. Google "mobile gyms" to bask in the creativity of other entrepreneurs for inspiration. See www.gymagic.com and www.mobilegymusa.com for examples.

Generally, a mobile studio will cost less than half of a small commercial storefront type of studio. Your biggest expense is the vehicle itself, which can range from $20,000 to $40,000 or more, depending on how elaborate you want to get. More and more

Zumba instructor Fabiola Moemi Marcial demonstrates in an open-air session for locals and tourists in Puerto Vallarta, Mexico.

businesses are going to their clients these days, but make sure your particular market will support this service and give you a sufficient return on your investment. A good approach would be to start by visiting your clients in their homes and offices; then, depending on their degree of interest, determine if they would use a mobile studio and be willing to pay proportionate fees.

The Great Outdoors

Parks, beaches, and wooded settings can provide inspirational atmosphere to your themed classes and work especially well for groups. Most often it is free to teach a class in a public setting, but the problem is that you can't reserve it. There are plenty of reservation options with boards of local park systems, though, and they come with perks that may help details of your event, such as having a kitchen readily available after your dance class for refreshment and snack preparation.

Community centers sometimes offer use of their attached sports fields and use of accompanying facilities for a fee. Consider how a beautiful, natural backdrop would affect your next class or one-to-one workout.

Commercial Facilities

Of course, you can open your own facility, targeted to clients who want personal service but don't want to join a traditional health club, gym, or spa. If you're going to invest in a commercial facility, be sure the market can support the business you envision. You need to calculate your investment; depending on the type of studio

The Franchise Option

If you're considering opening a studio, at least one company we came across offers franchise opportunities. Fitness Together has more than 340 locations throughout the United States and five countries. The concept involves one-on-one personal training in a private workout setting. For more information, visit http://corp.fitnesstogether.com.

and location, you'll need anywhere from $50,000 to $350,000 to furnish and equip your operation. Then figure out how much you can pay in cash and how much you're going to have to borrow. You'll need to do the market research to determine if you can generate sufficient business to service your debt and still operate your company. Whatever facility type you choose, you'll need to start connecting to health-focused markets. Work through the exercise on page 57 to jump-start that process.

The design of your facility is up to you. You might have one large open room with the various types of equipment grouped together. Or you might have several rooms

Beware!

The volume of music during group exercise classes should measure no more than 90 decibels (dB), and the instructor's voice should be about 10 dB louder—no more than 100 dB total—based on standards established by the Occupational Safety and Health Administration. A class C sound level meter can be purchased for under $100 and will provide a way to monitor sound to avoid damaging the hearing of your clients and instructors.

dedicated to specific functions, like a weight room and a cardiovascular equipment room.

Your clients will appreciate clean, spacious locker rooms with showers, toilets, sinks, and dressing areas, as well as a place for them to safely store their personal belongings. If your business is going to be a small studio where clients work primarily

Sad Brains Crave Fat

Research findings on the link between feeding oneself and emotions were reported in a 2011 American Society for Clinical Investigation article, "Fatty Acid-Induced Gut-Brain Signaling Attenuates Neural and Behavioral Effects of Sad Emotion in Humans." Findings proved the relationship between fat cravings and depression, or sadness, come from your brain. When the test brains were sad, they produced responses telling them they needed fat. Those neurological messages stop when the brain is happy. This exploration of the human body's messaging system of hunger, satiety, food intake, visceral sensory signaling, and emotions will provide insight into a wide range of disorders, including obesity, eating disorders, and depression. Read more of the findings on the *Journal of Clinical Investigation* site at: www.jci.org/articles/view/46380.

Team Up with the National Physical Activity Plan

The aim of the National Physical Activity Plan, a product of a private-public sector cooperative, is to increase Americans' physical activity through a comprehensive set of policies, programs, and initiatives.

With funding and focus to create a culture of health, there are many places within this plan that your creativity could pay off.

First read more about how hundreds of organizations are collaborating to facilitate fitness for this country at: www.physicalactivityplan.org.

Next, make a list of the businesses that appeal to you on the site.

1. _____

2. _____

3. _____

4. _____

5. _____

Finally, list ways to integrate your service with the businesses participating in this effort.

1. _____

2. _____

3. _____

4. _____

5. _____

The National Physical Activity Plan has a vision: One day, all Americans will be physically active and they will live, work, and play in environments that facilitate regular physical activity. Sharing a common vision with those who have funding is a smart way to make your business soar.

▲

under individual supervision, which means it will rarely be crowded, your locker rooms do not have to be able to accommodate more than a couple of people at a time.

The facility needs to have a sufficient number of electrical outlets if you are going to be using such machines as electric treadmills. Position equipment to provide a safe, comfortable environment for your clients. For cardiovascular equipment (treadmills, bicycles, elliptical machines, etc.), allow at least two to three feet of space between each machine. Clients need sufficient space to use the machines without interfering with another client. Have at least three feet of space behind each treadmill.

How Much Activity Is Enough?

A list of our nation's general health statistics generated by the combined U.S. health agencies and provided by www.fitness.gov include:

○ Adults 18 and older need 30 minutes of physical activity on five or more days a week to be healthy; children and teens need 60 minutes of activity a day for their health.

○ Significant health benefits can be obtained by including a moderate amount of physical activity (e.g., 30 minutes of brisk walking or raking leaves, 15 minutes of running, 45 minutes of playing volleyball). Additional health benefits can be gained through greater amounts of physical activity.

○ There are significant health benefits in taking 30 to 60 minutes of activity and breaking it down into smaller segments of 10 or 15 minutes throughout the day.

○ Moderate daily physical activity can reduce substantially the risk of developing or dying from cardiovascular disease, type 2 diabetes, and certain cancers, such as colon cancer. Daily physical activity helps to lower blood pressure and cholesterol, helps prevent or retard osteoporosis, and helps reduce obesity, symptoms of anxiety and depression, and symptoms of arthritis.

○ Heart disease is the leading cause of death among men and women in the United States. Physically inactive people are twice as likely to develop coronary heart disease as regularly active people.

○ 37 percent of adults report they are not physically active. Only 3 in 10 adults get the recommended amount of physical activity.

The free-weight area may be the most dangerous place in your facility. If your clients are not using the proper techniques, they could easily hurt themselves or someone else. Be sure they know how to safely handle weight plates, load a barbell, and handle dumbbells. Also, be sure you have adequate floor space for the clientele you'll be serving, and allow plenty of room between benches. The free-weight area should be supervised at all times, even though you may have clients who want to weight train on their own.

Attractive, friendly signage can help convey the standard of healthy, respectful behavior you expect from gym users. Making the message humorous with graphics can help.

Before designing your own facility, visit a substantial number of gyms, health clubs, and small studios to get ideas. Think carefully about the services you're going to provide and what type of environment will be most appropriate.

Think Personal Safety

Keep your personal safety in mind at all times. If you work with clients in their homes and offices, be cautious when you travel. Let someone else know your schedule, and consider checking in with that person on a regular basis. If you fail to check in, have a plan for what action they should take.

If you have a studio, be sure your reception desk is staffed at all times so people coming in and out are tracked. If you do not have sufficient personnel to do this, consider keeping the doors locked.

Medical Mysteries

Virtually every time you turn on your TV or pick up a newspaper, you'll see something about a new medical study that proves or disproves something. You can find studies that say caffeine is good for you and studies that say caffeine is bad for you. You can find studies that claim certain products or activities cause cancer and others that say those same products or activities are totally harmless. If you're confused, your clients are likely even more so.

Most people put a tremendous amount of faith in studies reported by the media. They are also often unable to recognize when someone with a legitimate medical degree is trying to sell them a dubious product, using a medical study as a sales technique. How can you sort out what's real and what's not? Here are some tips for evaluating medical studies:

○ *Find out if the study used animals or humans as subjects.* When studies use lab animals such as mice or rats, the results are not always relevant to human physiology.

○ *How many participants did the study include?* The more participants there were, the greater the chance that the results are valid. A good study will have at least 100 subjects.

○ *Where was the study published?* A peer-reviewed medical or scientific journal is a credible source.

○ *What was the geographic scope of the study and how many researchers were involved?* When tests are conducted only in one place by a small group of researchers, the chances for bias are higher than when multiple locations and more researchers are involved.

○ *Was there a control or placebo group?* Without a second such group, you won't know the true results.

○ *Are the findings ready for immediate application?* News reports of breakthroughs in weight control are common, but frequently the techniques are not available because more testing still needs to be done. Additional tests may disprove the theory.

Operating
in Cyberspace

The internet has changed the way many industries do business, and the fitness industry is no exception. Computer technology is opening up ways for trainers to expand their client base and stay connected with in-person clients. The internet continues to grow in popularity as more people become used to finding information online.

According to Pingdom (www.pingdom.com), a global internet monitoring firm, there were 1.97 billion internet users worldwide and 266.2 million in North America in June 2010.

So it's safe to assume that your clients and potential clients will expect you to have some kind of online presence. The computer face of your business is important because often it will be one of the first impressions your potential clients will have of you. There are several ways you can go online to enhance your marketing efforts, as well as generate supplemental sources of income. We'll give you some basic pointers in this chapter on creating a simple, business, online presence. It's in Chapter 6 that we'll really ask you to do some stretching (of the social media variety) and go beyond just setting up a website. You don't want to just get by doing the bare minimum, do you? Hurry up and get that website created so we can talk to you about blogging.

Setting Up Your Website

The simplest option is to create a website that functions primarily as an online brochure, giving clients information about your company and your trainers. This allows potential clients to learn about you in a relaxed, nonthreatening environment. "They can become interested and already sold on your facility even prior to coming in," explains Bill Sonnemaker, who owns a facility in Atlanta. "If they find something appealing about your website—if they like the content and the pictures—they'll feel more comfortable. And it provides credibility. When people call on the phone we always ask if they've had a chance to view our website."

One of the special features of Gunnar Peterson's website (www.gunnarpeterson. com) is a scrolling video montage on the homepage accompanied by dynamic music with celebrities crediting Peterson for their physiques. His appearances on lifestyle and entertainment, news, and fitness TV programs are featured in the mix and show portions of his workouts. Viewers can get a feel for his hard-driving, no shortcuts instruction style and sense of humor by watching. Another powerful feature on the site is a press section touting his uniqueness in health and fitness publications.

The special attributes of Tyrone Minor's site (www.chizelinc.com) are a cluster of impressive testimonials with dramatic before and after photos, a media section with snippets of Minor's appearances in various sports publications and websites, and a slick portfolio of his fitness modeling photography.

Some web hosting sites offer tools to quickly get your website up and running—for example, www.register.com and www.sitesell.com (which have tools to optimize your site so it will be picked up by search engines). You also can use these sites to check if your desired domain name is available.

Remember when designing every element of your site to make it as easy as possible for people to use. Here are some tips as you think about your site design:

- Determine how many pages you'll have and how you'd like to link them to each other.

- Make navigation easy—for example, users should be able to access major categories on your site from any page within the site.

- Imagine your typical audience member and what they're looking for. Create "gifts" for them in the form of knowledge. Short, newsy blasts of "Did you know?" style copy create interest for the viewer and make them want to linger on your site. Interesting photos that tell a story relevant to your business cause an attraction that can lead the viewer farther into your site.

- Pages, graphics, and blocks of copy should load quickly. If they don't, the user will leave.

- Only relevant information that the viewer will benefit from should be on each page. Anything else is distracting and uses up the viewer's attention span.

- Focus on keeping the design relatively simple and easy to read—avoid using big words when a friendly tone will do, and have enough blank space and/or graphics on the page so the reader isn't overwhelmed by text.

- Prominently display your contact information so users don't have to hunt for it—include contact names, your business name, address, phone, fax, and email.

Additionally, a potential client should be able to submit questions through a form on the website, as well as be able to email or call you. Remember that the form should be optional, and not the only way they can contact you. A properly designed form will allow you to obtain their contact information and use it later for newsletters and campaigns. Don't ask them to provide more information than an email address and phone number. If they can't call or email you, you may lose a sale. This kind of information capturing is fine if it's of service to the potential customer and lets them add details to their query, but if they can't just pick up the phone or shoot you an email because you've decided to only respond to messages, it smacks of customer service that will be for your convenience, not theirs.

Getting Outside Help

While you can design your own site, you'll save time by hiring outside help, and chances are you'll end up with a professional-looking design. Just make sure the

▲

designer builds in some flexibility so that you can make simple changes on your own, especially as your company grows. "As a small business, we wanted the ability to control the content and be able to update the site as necessary," says Bill S., who hired a designer for his company's site. "You don't

Bright Idea

To find a website designer, check with business and networking groups you belong to for references.

want to have employees listed who aren't with the business anymore. You don't want to offer or talk about things that are weeks old. That's why the ability to update—at no cost to us—is really beneficial. If we want to change a sentence, we're not dependent upon waiting for [a consultant] to have time, nor do we have to pay a $50 or $100 service fee to do that."

Here are more tips to keep in mind if you hire a web expert:

- When you come across a website you like, try to find out who the designer is (this is typically indicated at the bottom of the page). You also could simply ask the business directly.
- Keep favorite sites bookmarked so you'll be able to give the designer an idea of your preferences.
- As you're narrowing down your choice of designers, look at their own websites, and check out their portfolios.
- Consider putting your project out to bid online at www.guru.com, which is an online marketplace touting more than 600,000 freelancers whose expertise includes web design, programming, and graphic design.

Don't Give Away the Store

Be wary of putting too many exercise tips on your site—if you do so, keep things simple. This will help limit your potential liability and is just good marketing. "You want to give some information to be helpful so that even if they never contact you, perhaps you've motivated them, you've educated them," says Bill Sonnemaker. But from a sales standpoint, he says, giving away too much information for free isn't a good idea because the web surfer should have an incentive to contact you. In fact, that same principle applies to listing your prices. "One reason we don't publish our prices online," he says, "is that we at least want the opportunity to talk to them."

- Check to see if your designer can build the site from pre-formed templates—this could save on costs.
- If the developer is building the site from scratch, determine in writing who owns the source code—if the designer does, this could limit what you can do with the site later on.
- Get your agreement with the designer in writing and save your correspondence.

Computer-Based Training Tools

If you want to move beyond simply having a website presence, you could consider computer-based tools to enhance your services, either as your primary method of delivering training or in conjunction with face-to-face sessions.

Depending on the features of a particular program, you may be able to assess your clients' fitness levels, plan their programs, analyze their progress, maintain appointment schedules, handle billing and invoicing, and do training online. Online training allows you to give one-on-one attention to clients who may not be able to afford a face-to-face program, and to train clients in different geographic areas. Some services offer website setup. Here's a sampling of products, but shop around to find the personal trainer software or online service most appropriate for you:

Bright Idea

Computer software also is providing ways for you to stay organized and present a more professional image. Trainer Louis Coraggio uses a PDA-based personal training program from Vesteon Software (www.vesteon-software.com), which focuses on keeping detailed records of work-outs, billing, goals, and personal measurements for yourself or your clients. "Forget about clipboards and note taking," he says. "Use a program that is compatible with a PDA to document exercise data."

- Pro Fitness PT, www.profitnessprogram.com
- Visual ClubMate, www.aspensoftware.com
- BSDI, www.bsdiweb.com
- Hi-Tech Trainer, www.hitechwebflexor.com
- www.gubb.net
- www.pumpone.com
- Crosstrainer, www.crosstrainer.ca
- Wellcoaches, www.wellcoach.com

When Trainers Go Electronic

Trainer Mike Hood uses www.gubb.net to create, manage, and share an unlimited number of lists with clients. "It allows you to be mobile while not in a session, while integrating reminders, lists, and tips for various parts of everyday life," Hood says. Trainer Louis Coraggio uses www.pumpone.com, a membership site that helps you quickly set up an online training business. You get access to a drag and drop tool to create your own iPod workouts and an online store to sell them. "It is an effective way to increase clients and prevent burning out from trying to squeeze a certain amount of clients into a day," he says.

Another alternative is to design your own online training capability from scratch. Depending on how things are set up, clients could use your website to complete forms that would allow you to do an assessment and create a program for them. You could provide them with an online exercise diary, which you review regularly to evaluate their progress and make adjustments if necessary. Questions could be handled via email.

A good website designer should be able to set up an online personal training business site for you based on your specifications. Trainer Annette Hudson, for example, had her online training site (www.myfitnesstrainer.com) professionally designed. But it's not an inexpensive endeavor. "This cost a lot of money, which I funded with my [in person] personal training business," she says. "I won't quit training live until the website is making enough. If you are starting your own online company, you shouldn't expect it to make a lot of money right away."

Email Dos and Don'ts

Sending emails to your clients and prospects is an inexpensive way to stay connected. Bill S. sends out weekly or twice-weekly emails to his client list and people who have contacted the facility inquiring about services over the phone or through the website. "We send them information on current research findings, recipes, and other things related to health and fitness," he says. He often hears from people in other parts of the country who were forwarded one of his emails, and they request to get on his mailing list.

Research Insight

A new client may experience delayed onset muscle soreness (DOMS)—the pain from exercise that occurs 12 or more hours after training. This probably results from microscopic tearing of muscle fibers and swelling. Eccentric movements, such as running downhill or lowering weights, seem to be the worst culprits. Proper warm-up and cool-down can mitigate DOMS; once the damage is done, it may help to do low-impact cardio because this increases blood flow through the affected area.

But be cautious, because email can backfire in this day and age of spam email campaigns. "You've got to be careful because if you're soliciting, people are going to delete the mail and ask to be removed from your email list," Sonnemaker says. "Not one email we have sent out in the last three years said, 'Sign up now' or 'We've got this special going on.' Instead, we focus on educating."

Boosting Traffic

To drive traffic to your site, get creative. Trainer Annette Hudson, for example, ran a weight loss contest on her site. "I was rewarded with a dramatic increase in traffic," she says, "which continued after the contest ended. It was a lot of fun awarding the prizes, which were donated by Bowflex, PCGamerBike, AquaJogger, and others."

Another idea: If you have a membership website, you can give free trials to new members. "You'll dramatically improve your sign-up rate if you allow the member two weeks to make sure they like the program," says Hudson. She also suggests giving website members inexpensive gifts that display your logo, such as pens and calendars.

Here are more traffic-boosting strategies:

- When you use a program such as Google AdWords, an ad for your website appears next to internet search results based on keywords you choose. You're charged when someone clicks on your ad. "I recommend using the most specific keywords that you can—this will keep the cost way down," Annette says. "For example, if your studio is located in Minneapolis, use the keywords 'Minneapolis personal training' instead of 'personal training.'"

- Use a free online search engine submission tool so the search engines will find your site. The hosting and site-building service at www.sitesell.com has user-friendly tools for search engine optimization.

- Issue a press release about your new site and include the address on all of your stationery, business cards, and brochures.

- Offer to exchange links with other websites that are complementary to yours—you'll list their link on your site if they list your link on theirs.

We'll talk more about this in Chapter 6.

Stat Fact

According to Les Mills International's 2009 "Future of Fitness White Paper," approximately 15 million new gym memberships are sold in the U.S. each year, but 12 million members are also lost each year. Nearly one in four leave their club within the first year of joining. Read more of this study at: www.futureoffit-nesswhitepaper.com.

Website Disclaimer

As the number of people who use the internet to find information and conduct business increases, so does the volume of related litigation. Disclaimers can help minimize the potential liability from the use of your site.

If you provide links to other online merchants, consider including a disclaimer that you are not endorsing the products or services sold on the linked site, nor are you responsible for the quality or performance of those products or services. If you provide any type of healthcare advice or information, your disclaimer should identify the source of the information and state that use of the information is not a substitute for medical treatment. It's a good idea to consult with an attorney to make sure the type, content, and locations of your disclaimers are appropriate and effective.

6

Create Social Media Presence in 19 Baby Steps

The very best use of social media for the benefit of your business follows the customer service phrases, "How can I help you?" and "What can I do for you?" If you keep asking those questions as you get comfortable with and make use of social media tools, you're halfway to harnessing that beautiful mix of online socializing, marketing, and the in-person events that bring it all together.

The other part of the equation is making sure you position yourself to online search engines as an attractive source so they'll promote you and people will be able to find you, but we'll get to that later. Back to the primary focus of this chapter—we can't stress it enough and it bears repeating: "How can I help you? What can I do for you?" That sentiment should shine through each and every tool and method you use.

Making Use of Heavy Traffic Sites

Imagine singing a wonderful opera in a subway tunnel and the meager handful of coins you'd earn, dropped into your hat as you warbled away like Pavarotti. That would be because most people bustling through a subway aren't educated opera fans, weren't walking down the tunnel seeking entertainment, didn't have extra pocket change for you, or simply weren't interested in your gift. This scene relates to what can happen if you have wonderful products and services and put them in front of the wrong audience. What a waste of your time and energy it would be to invest in creating your online presence in the wrong spot, in a "room" full of people who didn't understand your value.

Where's My Tribe?

All of the work you do online, whether writing or creating video for others' blogs or your own various sites, should be placed in high-traffic areas made up of the kind of people who are looking for services like yours.

Who are those people? Which websites do they frequent? These questions are yours to answer with research, depending on the niche you fall into. We recommend looking for the most used social media sites and then determining what the biggest user demographic is on those sites and targeting that group. For example, because Digg users are 60 percent male and between the ages of 18 and 24, it would not be the best place to attract clients if your campaign is for menopausal women who've tried everything else and just can't get the weight off. For reasons you see in the list below, Classmates and possibly Facebook would better serve you for a campaign like that.

Here's a rundown of some of the major players out there in the speedily growing world of social media:

www.Facebook.com

- 125 million unique monthly visitors during peaks
- 61 percent age 35 and older

- 55 percent female users
- Social information exchange
- Most popular social networking site

www.Digg.com

- 8.5 million unique monthly visitors during peaks
- Most popular with age group 18–24
- 60 percent male users
- Provides a sharing venue for news, video, photos
- Submissions are voted to popularity by users

www.Slashdot.com

- 10 thousand unique monthly visitors during peaks
- Most popular with age group 25–34
- 82 percent male users
- News and stories exchange

www.LinkedIn.com

- Over 15 million unique monthly visitors during peaks
- Most popular with age group 35–44
- 52 percent male users
- Business and professional network and referrals

www.Classmates.com

- Over 18 million unique monthly visitors during peaks
- Most popular with ages 55 and up
- 64 percent female users
- Connection site for former classmates

www.Bebo.com

- 3.5 million unique monthly visitors during peaks
- Most popular with age group 18–24
- 66 percent female
- Basic social networking site
- Social information exchange

www.Meetup.com

- 3 million unique monthly visitors during peaks
- Most popular with age group 45–54
- 57 percent female users
- Hobbyists, special-interest groups connector, for meeting in person

www.Twitter.com

- Over 28 million unique monthly visitors during peaks
- Most popular with age group 25–34
- 55 percent female users
- Information and announcement platform
- Limited character capacity requires brief or abbreviated statements

www.Yelp.com

- Over 38 million unique monthly visitors during peaks
- Most popular with age group 25–34
- 55 percent female users
- Exchange site for business service reviews by location and rating

Baby Steps

Don't feel overwhelmed. It's a lot to take in. The fact that we'd like you to create a presence on at least five of those sites might have you hyperventilating, but when you break it down into baby steps it boils down to a relaxing nightly habit of 15 minutes with a nice cup of tea.

Here are the steps we recommend you take to get started finding the crowd who will understand your value and begin attracting them.

1. Do some research on your very specific target audience and create a list of where they spend their time on- and offline. Go to www.city-data.com and www.google.com/trends to start word searching your market.

Smart Tip

Tip...

Every time you name a blog, photo, video, web page, or article, you should use words that your audience will be searching with. You should also try to include those words within the body of your articles. Those words are like hooks for the search engines to grab you with.

Make a list of your market's qualities and keep it handy.

2. Search online for blogs relating to the subject matter you just uncovered in step one. Bookmark the sites or add their links to your "favorites" folder.

3. Write a list of ten topics related to your industry that you're knowledgeable on.

4. Write a list of ten problems that your audience has and convert those problems into article topics peppered with your knowledge.

> **Smart Tip**
>
> Give magazine subscriptions to your major clients for Valentine's Day to celebrate their hearts. Magazines focusing on whole health topics will provide subject matter for them to engage you in related to their program goals and give them context for the education you provide.

5. Buy an inexpensive digital camera with video—at least 5 megapixel capability. This shouldn't cost more than $90. The Kodak Easyshare is a reliable, easy-to-use camera and is about $80 and less on sale.

6. Go to www.wordpress.com and set up a blog. Use some of the sharp widgets at www.prnewswire.com/bloggers/services to make your blog spiffy and attention-getting.

7. Go to www.youtube.com and set up a channel.

8. Go to Facebook and set up a business page, not a personal page. Pepper it with photos, a business bio, and a few short articles about your goals.

9. Consider the information you've collected in steps one through four and pick a topic from the list of your audience's problems. Turn it into a catchy article title that would capture your demographic interest. For example, you could address the single parents among your audience who have trouble getting a babysitter for their kids with an article titled, "Working Out with Your Kids Can Teach Great Habits."

   Be creative in the article and talk about how parents can empower their kids to be coaches, riding their bikes while the parent jogs, cheering them on, and the benefits of doing this activity together.

   Your article only need be two or three paragraphs and shouldn't take more than 15 minutes to write. You've got 20 articles to write, so make it snappy and don't choose topics you know nothing about!

   Now, either take photos that relate to your topic or use a stock photography site and choose some nice images to complement your article. Just search "royalty free photos" and you'll find sites offering free and low-cost images.

10. Repeat this process until you have about ten articles with accompanying images, and post them in an organized fashion on your Wordpress blog. Make

sure to take advantage of the attractive features Wordpress offers, like stylized backgrounds, widgets that link your other online profiles to your blog, and subscriber buttons.

If you put a subscriber button on your blog, you'll be notified each time someone subscribes and they, in turn, will get an email alert each time you post another fascinating article. This is a good way to stay connected to people who are interested in what you do. Later when you have something else to tell them about, such as an event or contest, you have all of their emails right there.

11. Get that camera out and make a tutorial on one of your signature exercises and post it on your YouTube profile. Make sure to give it a catchy title. Repeat this until you have ten videos. Of course, you can also create tutorials with photo stills and insert them singly on your blog or insert them into a slideshow program on a photo-sharing site such as www.flickr.com or www.shutterfly.

Massive Exposure Never Hurts

Here is a list of additional video sites you can post your genius video creations on for even more exposure:

Blip.tv—http://blip.tv

Blip TV reaches millions of viewers by syndicating its content with Twitter, Facebook, AOL Video, Yahoo! Video, MySpace, MSN Video, and Google Video.

www.vimeo.com

Vimeo lets you control who sees your videos and gives lots of pointers for optimizing them to their highest potential technical quality.

www.saymedia.com

This site allows users to share videos via email, direct HTML embedding, and permalinks, and has a snazzy interface; if you get major hits on your fantastic workout videos, you may be eligible to make some money with them.

This is a list of 31 additional video sites to post on: http://chaos-laboratory.com/2007/08/30/top-31-free-alternatives-to-youtube-video-hosting-sites.

com. If you use photos you have taken of other people in your post, you may want to use the Model Release form we have provided on page 82.

Take a look at these links to see good examples of instruction coupled with displaying proper form in a linear style, and videos with narration:

www.acefitness.org/exerciselibrary

www.facebook.com/pages/Fitness-Tutorials/220803844652699

12. Cross-reference all of your sites to one another. Your Facebook site should contain a brief profile of your business, some great photos, a few videos, and three or four sentences or headline teasers that link to the articles on your blog. Your YouTube channel should contain teasers leading to your blog and Facebook page, and so on.

13. Do a word-specific search on Google that expresses what your audience is looking for. In other words, pretend you are them, looking for you. Look at the top 20 sites that come up. Look at each one, and if it is or has a blog within it, read a bit, and then contact the blogger to see if you may post a link to their site on yours and ask if you may submit an article to them to post. They may say no. Sometimes it's best to just ask if you can feature them on your site and wait to see if they return the favor. If not, move on to the next site.

14. Now that you have some snazzy online presence, it's time to get out into the real world and complete the circle with actual, face-to-face networking. We don't want you to just stand in a room, drink wine, and talk politics. We want you to find a group of people who are already interested in fitness or being very active, join them in their activities, and offer to help them. You can help other people while you're helping yourself.

15. Look up fitness-related events in your city on www.meetup.com. Choose a couple of groups with a lot of members and start to go to their events regularly.

Bring your camera and take photos of the event. If you feel the need to ask permission to do this, go ahead, but because Meetup is a social organization, events are photographed by multiple participants for fun, and if they aren't, people seem to always want more photos to be taken. If it's a hike in the woods or a trail run, get nice photos of the physicality and nature.

Tell the group moderator and guests at the event that you'll be posting the photos on your blog and then hand them a card with your blog address on it. People will tune in to look at the group photos and see all of your top-notch fitness tutorials and be impressed. At the next meeting they'll probably start asking you about your services.

You can repeat this process with other fitness social groups.

16. Go to www.yelp.com and create a business profile replete with photos, a crisp, dynamic bio, and links back to your other sites.

17. List a low-cost or free social exercise event on Yelp that will be held in a beautiful outdoor venue, such as a nature preserve or city park.

    Remember to use key words when listing your event. Try to host one of these each month so that guests can get to know one another. At these events they'll learn about your other fitness offerings.

18. The circle closes by starting at the beginning—in-person networking can be greatly complemented before or after events by using blogs and social connection sites such as Yelp, Meetup, and Facebook to:
    - Brief members on news about the group
    - Show off photos of the event
    - Announce future engagements and speakers
    - Re-engage group members on related topics for further online discussion
    - Expose group members to elements of your business that would help them (if those elements relate to what people need or want)
    - Post industry news links from other sites
    - Review products, services, and places your audience uses

---

Themed Fitness Events for Niche Audiences

- ○ Ladies Night Out, City Night Hikes with Weights
- ○ Workout with Your Toddler
- ○ Love Me, Love My Dog: Aerobics with Fido
- ○ Baby Boomer 50s Dance Workout
- ○ Single Parents Pilates at the Beach
- ○ Saturday Morning Dance Party and Coffee
- ○ Snowshoe Racing
- ○ Campsite Breakfast and Hike
- ○ Grocery Store Tours, How to Shop Healthy
- ○ Paddleboard and Picnic

19. Now is the time to blow your trumpet to everyone you know. Show off all of your hard work on the internet by inviting all of your contacts to experience particular aspects of your profile. Be specific and write a personal email to each person that says something like, "I know you like yoga, so I thought you'd appreciate this," and send them the link to the related article on your blog. Or send one of your core exercise tutorials on YouTube to someone who is struggling with that area of strength building.

Words Are Hooks

When people go online to search for things related to fitness, they use specific search words. Additionally, different audiences may use different words to search for similar things. Word choices are directly related to the challenges or problems each group faces. Put yourself in their shoes and ask, "If this is my problem, then what am I searching for to alleviate it?" Those will lead you to that group's word choices. See the Search Word Worksheet on page 78.

How Are the Pros Using Social Media?

Each of the professionals in this book are using social media as a tool to get to the next level with their businesses. Some are encouraged by their web designers, and others are experimental by nature, so trying out tools on the web seems essential and fun.

Gunnar Peterson still considers himself a newbie when it comes to using social media to promote his business. He was instructed by a client to work with Twitter to create a following to prep the launch of a product and knows he should continue in that vein. He's trying to make time for it and slowly getting there.

Pat Henry uses social media tools to demonstrate exactly what her service is since it is unusual. One of the greatest challenges is getting people committed to letting go of preconceptions, because they are so conditioned to working in their heads and thinking too much about what they are doing. It is more difficult to learn to improvise than to pursue a set routine. As a new fitness practice, which has no frame of reference as does Zumba, for example, Organic Stretching™ is best promoted via free introductory demonstrations, which Henry offers monthly at her studio as well as off-site.

By showing how the practice works and what it's done for her and others, documenting those successes via testimonials in articles on her blog and Facebook,

Search Word Worksheet

One thing you can do is to make sure every venue where you showcase yourself online is loaded with search words that enable people to find you. We've given you a list below of audience types and some of the challenges they face. Your assignment right now is to imagine and write down the words that each would use to search for fitness-related services.

Group	Challenges	Word Search Choices
Stay-at-home moms	Pressed for time Need a babysitter Hard to eat healthy when cooking for the whole family	
Single parents	May want to meet other singles with kids Possibly babysitter-challenged Could be facing financial challenges	
Injured or recovering surgery patients	Fear of pain from exercising Possibly in need of transportation Feeling vulnerable	
Cancer or autoimmune-challenged patients	Nausea Partially immobile	
Professional athletes	Need to get to the next fitness level Plateauing	
Baby boomers	Empty nest syndrome Might have trouble meeting people	
Sufferers of depression	Don't want to leave the house	

Smart Tip

Tyrone Minor from Chizel Inc. has several memberships at gyms where he meets clients for training. He learned not to conduct his own personal workout at any of those gyms because clients would walk up to him and start asking for advice, putting him in a position to either give away his services for free or face refusing the customer. He chose to simply take himself out of that equation.

circulating her video, and conducting private workshops upon request, Henry attracts new clients, an especially hard feat in a tourist area such as Puerto Vallarta, where people may just be visiting for a week.

Diana Broschka says, "I use Facebook to drive connections to our website by suggesting they become fans. We also both use Twitter and Facebook as education and information vehicles, sharing information with clients and prospective clients to build credibility and trust. We use them to post training schedules, [acknowledge] client birthdays and other relationship-building messages, as well." Broschka uses Facebook and Twitter to connect to other credible fitness businesses and institutions as a means of staying current on industry events and news.

"Since Facebook and Twitter are free, it is important for us to use them consistently and regularly to promote our gym and services. We have utilized Facebook paid advertising with some success. While LinkedIn may not be considered social media, we use it as a means to establish professional credibility for owners—we share this and make it available for transparency," Broschka concludes. Search "Diana Broschka" on Twitter, Facebook, and LinkedIn to see how she's positioned her company, 501FIT.

For finding the right people to employ and redirect traffic back to 501FIT's website, Broschka uses LinkedIn and Facebook. "We have also utilized LinkedIn to promote the gym via job openings or positions for hire," she says. We also use the newsfeeds on Facebook to tag along to the posts of other organizations to again redirect attention back to our gym and services."

Tyrone Minor says that if you advertise your services on places like Craigslist, you'll attract the kind of customers who either can't or won't pay you what your time is worth because it's a site where people are looking for deals. He suggests instead focusing on using Facebook to grow your audience by conveying the quality of what you do. You can showcase your talents, education, qualifications, and tutorials on Facebook to build credibility and attract

Smart Tip

Encourage your clients to review your services on www.citysearch.com and www.yelp.com. Here's an example of 501FIT's high ratings and reviews on City Search: http://twincities.citysearch.com/profile/46283047/minneapolis_mn/501fit_g_werx.html.

attention. Minor says what you can charge is influenced by the results you help your clients achieve, your ability to motivate them, and the array of services you provide, as well as your qualifications. You can showcase all of that through blogs and various site appearances and contributions, as well as in-person networking.

Good Habits Die Hard

They say if you do anything for 21 days, it becomes a habit. Here's an opportunity to take the discipline you apply to your body and harness it to give your business a social makeover, get more clients, attract a specific demographic, change the way people view fitness, and express your talents in a new venue.

If you choose to do this homework just 20 minutes a day, you'll be working toward something that doesn't cost a penny and can't cost a penny, because it can't be purchased. It's an earned profile that you illuminate your business with by giving generously and wisely, investing some "relationship" time, and show up for routinely and long term.

What are we talking about here? This is really a simple matter of sharing—much like you would in a phone conversation with a friend—advice or support in areas you see them struggling. You've got to be physically comfortable while working on your computer to make this something you'll want to do every night. Think again of a phone conversation with a friend, and for those of you who hate talking on the phone, think of sitting in a wine bar, coffee shop, or around a campfire.

Building Relationships Takes Time

Remember that knowledge is a gift. In order for people to equate the value of what you give them to what it's actually worth, you may have to wait for results. They need to let it sink in and get to know you. They also need to see your face and get involved, which is why the in-person part of the equation can't be skipped.

Just like with fitness, participating successfully in social media to build social capital is more of a lifestyle than an exercise you do for quick results.

These steps can be taken slowly in segments, in short blocks of time to get you to the end goal of creating a large following online that can't wait to read what you write. Now go on. They're waiting for you.

Home School for Savvy

Stock your shelves with a rounded education from the social media and customer service experts. Leave books all over the house for quick, ten-minute information grabs that will influence your behavior:

○ *Built to Serve: How to Drive the Bottom Line with People First Practices* by Dan J. Sanders, United Supermarkets Ltd., McGraw-Hill

○ *Engage! The Complete Guide for Brands and Businesses to Cultivate and Measure Success in the New Web* by Brian Solis, John Wiley and Sons Inc.

○ *Delivering Happiness: A Path to Profits Passion and Purpose* by Tony Hsieh, Business Plus, Hachette Book Group, www.hachettebookgroup.com

○ *Entrepreneur* Magazine, Entrepreneur Media, Inc., www.entrepreneur.com

○ *Facebook Marketing: Leverage Social Media to Grow Your Business* by Steven Holzner, Que Publishing

○ *How to Increase Your Website Traffic* by Khoa Bui, Entrepreneur Press

○ *How to Make Money with YouTube* by Brad and Debra Schepp, McGraw-Hill

○ *The Celebrity Assistant's Handbook: How to Successfully Work With Celebrities, Billionaires, and the Top One Percent* by C.S. Copeland, www.personalassistant guide.com

○ *The Everything Guide to Social Media* by John K. Waters, Adams Media, www.everything.com

○ *The Thank You Economy* by Gary Vaynerchuk, HarperCollins Publishers

○ *The Tipping Point: How Little Things Can Make a Big Difference* by Malcolm Gladwell, Backbay Books

○ *Who* by Geoff Smart and Randy Street, ghSMART and Company Inc., Random House

○ *Zingerman's Guide to Giving Great Service* by Ari Weinzweig, Hyperion

Get Them to Sign on the Dotted Line

If you feature photos on your sites with clients in them, have them sign a release. Anyone else that isn't you needs to sign one of these, even if they give verbal permission. It could serve as smart protection later.

Model Release

I hereby give permission to [insert your company name] and [insert your name] to use my photos and likeness in all forms and media for advertising, portfolio, demo, trade, stock photography, editorial, altering without restrictions, and all other lawful purposes targeted toward the production and promotion of [your business name]. I understand I am entitled to no compensation. I release [your name] from all forms of claims and liability related to my photo usage.

Date: _____

Print Name: _____

Signature: _____

Setting Yourself Apart

The challenges facing clients are many: time constraints, stress, aging, and terrible food options at grocery stores and restaurants, to name a few. The National Weight Loss Registry creates control groups to study weight loss success. A breakdown of the habits of "successful losers" shows that 78 percent eat breakfast every day, 62 percent watch less than ten hours of TV per week, and 90 percent exercise at least an hour per day. As you know, those percentages do not reflect the habits of most people, which is why millions of people continue to struggle with obesity, despite the media attention on the problems associated with weight gain. At the same time, our sedentary lifestyle has led to muscle and postural imbalances and a loss of functional strength.

Fortunately, the health and fitness industry is evolving to meet these challenges. While that means you have to adapt with the changes to stay competitive and attract clients, it also means that opportunities to grow your business are never in short supply. And with so much happening in the field, you'll always be assured that your work will be exciting and inspiring.

Trends

Trends are created to answer a need that observant entrepreneurs notice. Are you one of them? Can you take the best of many forms and create something new? It has been said that there is no such thing as new art because everything created now is by experiencing something else and then mocking it with a spin.

Gunnar Peterson says, "People used to tell me not to give away my proprietary programs and exercises, but everything in the exercise business is poached. Everyone poaches to create their own methods. It's not important that people poach. Poaching doesn't make you a bad person and it can make you a better trainer. What is important is what they wind up doing with the material."

Peterson studies everything from pilates to powerlifting, the movements of runners, and many other athletic disciplines to create his own unique configurations. "In addition to uniquely combining movements, the way you time and

Gunnar Peterson with exercise ball.

sequence them really matters," he says. You can pepper a new sequence or different ingredient into a workout and create a completely different response."

Here we highlight trends that offer an opportunity for you to enhance your training business. Realize that by thinking creatively, analyzing forecasts, and emerging trends, and being open to new ideas, you'll begin to see new possibilities for your talents. Look to the future and imagine yourself the pioneer of a new trend to add to this list for extra motivation.

Zumba

Though Zumba is capitalized by the originator and those who become certified by Zumba Fitness™, the term "zumba" is used generically to define Latin-style, high-energy dance exercise.

Launched in the early 1990s, zumba has grown exponentially, with millions of people now attending classes in well over one hundred countries. This wildly popular, easy-to-follow dance fitness program is the brain child of three entrepreneurial Colombians, one of whom, Alberto Beto Perez, accidentally created what has now become the rage.

A South American fitness instructor and celebrity trainer and choreographer, Beto one day inadvertently left behind the traditional aerobics music he used to teach his students and improvised during class with his native tunes featuring salsa, samba, and merengue rhythm styles.

Using the tapes he had with him in his backpack, he combined the pulsating Latin beats with international dance steps, and Zumba Fitness™ came into being. Zumba Fitness™ is the founding organization that named, trademarked, and propelled the program to global popularity through dissemination of DVDs, infomercials, and, subsequently, formal training and certification for professional instructors.

Sessions are held at health clubs, gyms, auditoriums, yoga studios, and warm climates and travel destinations, often in the open air, on the beach, in local parks, public squares, and at sports arenas.

According to 20-year-old Puerto Vallarta zumba instructor Fabiola Noemi Marcial, in an effort to help the population combat obesity, the local government provides financial assistance to aspiring zumba teachers, offering monetary support with their training, certification, and subsequent teaching income. After honing her skills as a zumba student for five years, she became certified and now teaches two high-energy hourlong classes per day, five days a week. Since becoming an instructor six months ago she has shed several pounds, an added benefit to making money doing something she loves.

A uniformly hued mass of humanity, zumba dancers number in the hundreds and sway in unison to the beat, mesmerizing bystanders.

As part of their community health initiative, Puerto Vallarta officials organize and host mass zumba parties, typically held in huge spaces such as popular retail store parking lots, including Costco's, and the picturesque seaside malecon (boardwalk) that can accommodate any and all interested zumba students and teachers within the municipality. For up to three hours every other month, a group of a dozen or so instructors lead participants in familiar steps learned in weekly classes. The event is free, but registration is required. In addition to providing current students/teachers with an opportunity to practice their zumba skills, the highly visible event is a very effective marketing device to attract new participants, who are eager to become part of the crowd having so much fun together.

Zumba classes are usually an hour long, and U.S. prices range from approximately $15 to $25, which are typically included in most health club memberships. Instructors can earn as much as $40 per hourlong class, depending on several factors, such as their student following, experience teaching, and number of certifications.

They can operate as an independent, securing and renting their own teaching space, or provide their services under the umbrella of an established fitness facility. The latter may pay less but typically provides the instructor with greater liability protection.

According to a survey released by the American College of Sports Medicine, zumba placed in the top ten fitness trends for 2012. The ACSM survey collects data from more than 2,600 fitness professionals and is designed to identify trends ranging from career opportunities to target client groups, in order to assist the fitness industry in making future business decisions.

Whether an actual trend or a passing fad, zumba has become one of the fastest growing dance-based fitness crazes in the country. As evidenced by zumba's typically eclectic class profiles, people of all ages and fitness levels are drawn to its infectious music, easily replicated dance moves, and weight-loss, body-toning benefits.

To accommodate various populations and special needs (such as clients with muscular dystrophy and in wheelchairs), the basic zumba program has spawned several variations, including: zumba for baby boomers in which moves are modified and the pace slowed down a bit without compromising the Latin flavor; zumba toning and sculpting; aqua zumba, which provides a water-based workout; zumba for kids; and zumba combined with circuit and resistance training, to name a few.

Successfully completing the workshop provides the attendee with a license good for one year, which must be renewed thereafter by updating skills. Certification for the specialized zumba courses entails further training. An ideal background for an aspiring instructor is one of dance and fitness, with prior practical exposure to zumba as a student very helpful. A variety of training/certifying options and other pertinent information can be found at www.zumbadance.com.

Salvador Mascarenas Ruiz, 45, has been in the profession since 1990 and is a sought-after, charismatic trainer whose work schedule is staggering. Most days average five classes, ranging from body pump, circuit, and specialty glutes and abs work, to salsa fitness (a variation of zumba), six days a week.

Despite his passion and natural affinity for dancing, at 6'1" and 250 pounds, Ruiz told us he didn't "fit [visually] into traditional dance troupes." Nonetheless, he used his skills to earn an income choreographing quinceañeras, a very popular Hispanic tradition rite of passage celebration for 15-year-old girls. Eventually, cast in a play that required him to learn the basics of jazz, he took workshops through which he ultimately discovered aerobics, and fell immediately in love with this rhythmic exercise modality.

Destination Venues

Mascarenas Ruiz brings his expertise to whatever venue his clients prefer—their home, the beach, the gym, or a park. "If the client isn't happy and comfortable in his/

her workout environment, he/she will not succeed," he says. Exercise is very personal, and every client and teacher is unique. The goal of every student—whatever the age or gender—is "more happiness, achieved by getting more fit. My job is to help them to feel and look better, modifying every movement I teach to the varying abilities of the individual."

Ruiz has witnessed fitness trends come and go, with spinning and zumba very popular classes most recently. On the horizon, he anticipates clients having a greater interest in TRX (portable resistance and suspension training) and working out in natural surroundings.

Group Training

Group training includes many variations and fulfills social needs, provides a feeling of freedom and anonymity, and often is a way for people to pay a noncommittal, small fee for a fun workout. It also provides variety and an aerobic balance for those who are training seriously with weights or other strength building methods.

Phil Martens developed a machine called G-Werx Gym (www.gwerx.com), which is a full workout station and allows trainers to personally train up to ten clients (on ten machines) simultaneously in one compact area. 501F1T uses the G-Werx Gym free weight cardio system to get the most indelible results for clients while they work in a group setting, creating a group-trainer camaraderie. "There is a trainer in the class all the time, but he or she only helps clients one-to-one if they need it. The group facet of this training helps clients afford a long-term fitness solution to needed lifestyle changes," Martens says.

In each of Pat Henry's Organic Stretching™ classes, she guides one section of the practice, has students work solo, then teams them up with one partner and finally the entire group to utilize others' bodies to work against.

Virtually anyone can benefit from Henry's method; her own clientele ranges in age from late

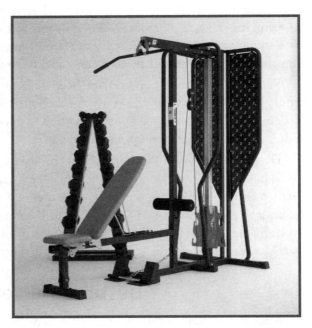

G-Werx Gym designed and patented by Phil Martens

Organic Stretching™ students Andrea Kast and Florelisa Hernandez Sanchez team up during class, and utilize each other's body to release upper back and shoulder tension.

40s to 80s, many of whom have experienced significant improvement with long-term and episodic lower back, shoulder, knee, and sciatica issues. Classes are an hour long and meet twice weekly.

Zumba enthusiasts liken their exercise experience to partying with a group of friends. Groups, parties, events, and classes are melding together in the trend of group training, which provides a way for people to meet in a no-pressure setting and "let it all out." Friends made in a setting like this get to know one another quickly, because it's hard to be shy or seem mysterious when there are nonstop high-energy movements and perspiration-drenched workout clothes involved. Along with the fun social element, there is a huge sense of personal and esteem-building satisfaction in having moved aerobically—virtually nonstop—for nearly an hour. The camaraderie of "dancing" together as a multilegged ensemble of all ages and sizes soon builds a micro fitness community of zumba devotees.

With tag lines such as "Ditch the workout, join the party," and "Party yourself into shape," the appeal of zumba is widespread, attracting predominantly women. One of several plusses of zumba is that it does not require a partner, as many dance genres do, or any special equipment of participants or instructors. In addition, it is noncompetitive, so a participant can move at his or her own pace, even just shifting in place, until familiar with the basic moves, without feeling awkward or embarrassed.

Hundreds of zumba devotees gather in the open air for extended dance/exercise marathons on Puerto Vallarta's scenic malecon (boardwalk) alongside the Bay of Banderas.

Instructors are certified to lead basic zumba after a one-day training course that teaches the fundamental steps and rhythms, and typically costs between $225 and $285.

TRX

TRX is a full-body workout program and product that utilizes a system of high-tension straps. The straps can be attached to a tree limb, pull-up bar, or door for the workout. Part of the appeal and popularity is the convenience of being able to both take the portable kit almost anywhere and also get in a strenuous workout that targets all the major muscle groups, and in 25 minutes. The kits are as affordable as a gym membership and very convenient for busy people. See www.trxtraining.com.

Yoga, Stretching Arts, and Preventative Therapy

There are many types of yoga, from the fast, warm methods such as Bikram, Power, and Vinyasa, to the version that focus on extreme bending and stretching such as Ashtanga and Forrest, but strength and flexibility are at the core of all of them. Creating a unique version of their own based on the best of what they've experienced has been the road to success for many of our entrepreneurs.

Improvisation is integral to the system Pat Henry developed, although to an observer, it appears otherwise. There are no set movements, per se, or positions as with most practices, such as tai chi or yoga. The entire focus is on connective tissue, especially joints, and the goal is to increase range of motion, which is an asset no matter what one's exercise regimen or how optimal one's fitness level.

She designed Organic Stretching™ not only to help mitigate or eliminate existing injuries, but also assist in preventing them down the road. Henry believes the body has a "deep knowing," with respect to what it needs, but the head gets in the way and says something else. The movements Henry teaches seem unusual, and reminiscent of the seemingly limitless feats most people did naturally as infants. (Does lying on your back, cooing contentedly in your crib, and effortlessly nibbling on your toes ring a bell?)

A Lush Take on Discipline

Rock star Madonna recently opened a worldwide chain of innovative global gyms called Hard Candy Fitness. In conjunction with Mark Mastrov, the creator of 24-Hour Fitness, her manager Guy Oseary, and New Evolution Ventures (NEV), Madonna brought her ideal, formulated from using gyms around the world, to the drawing table and created a masterpiece that promises to "make working out sexy, cool and fun while producing head-turning results." Answering the call of emerging trends in combining socializing, dance, virtual, and tech, Hard Candy is a one-of-a-kind experience, which merges entertainment with fitness through:

- ○ Lavish surroundings
- ○ Creative artwork and music from Madonna's favorite artists
- ○ Luxurious lounge areas
- ○ Motivational sound and light experiences
- ○ Zumba
- ○ Latin moves
- ○ Capoeria

A Lush Take on Discipline, continued

○ Kickboxing

○ Bike studio

○ BarWorks

○ Mind body studio

○ Sculpting

○ Sauna and steam rooms

○ State-of-the-art cardio equipment

○ Group fitness

○ Phone coaching

○ Access to calorie and activity management system, recipes, and exercise videos

○ Emerging trends

Hard Candy Fitness boasts some of the best personal trainers and dancers in the industry.

"Our goal is to create an environment inspired by Madonna's vision and high standards of what the ideal gym would be. Hard Candy Fitness will be a reflection of Madonna's point of view and will reflect her input on every detail, including music, space, light, and other design cues. Madonna's touch will be everywhere," states NEV chairman Mark Mastrov.

See www.hardcandyfitness.com and www.madonna.com for the rest of the story.

"We were born with a high level of internal fluidity," Henry says, "but as the years pile up, the tissues dry out in areas we don't move routinely. We overlook and accommodate limitations, often unaware that we are not operating at 100 percent. We move mechanically—seldom with much rotation, especially in our spines—and eventually lose mobility in our hips and other joints." Organic Stretching™ helps one to experience the full capacity intended in the joints and optimize range of motion, which Henry maintains is not the same as flexibility. The latter is about elongating muscles; the former, restoring/enhancing rotation of our joints.

One key principle of Organic Stretching™, among several, is that every movement undertaken has support. In the case of an injured shoulder, for example, an individual would utilize his/her arm to lift the other and ease the weight of that limb, enhancing mobility in the affected shoulder, pumping lymph fluid and eliminating toxins from that joint. Initially students in her classes follow the movements demonstrated by Henry, who coaches them into "places they wouldn't go on their own," until their bodies learn the physical possibilities, every one of which has potential benefits. Just by making tiny adjustments—exploring one's leg with the back of one's hand vs. the palm, as one would typically do, for example, the body's structural components and circuitry are rearranged. If you take any part of your body that you can move, such as your elbow, and move it anywhere it can reach along the surface of your body, you have done miraculous things for your joints in the process.

Some clients substitute Henry's program for their traditional fitness regimens, while others use it to supplement swimming, dance, etc. Her goal is to teach others the system so they can train their own clients.

Baby Boomer Fitness

Youthful-looking, 60-year-old Barbara Crompton predominantly attracts clients—both men and women—between the ages of 40 and 60-plus. Younger would-be students generally have the misconception that classes taught by an "older" teacher will not be challenging enough. However, on the occasion that a 20-something individual does take her Vinyasa class, for example, he/she soon learns that chronological age is not necessarily a valid indicator of a teacher's level of physicality.

Crompton supplements weekly classes with twice-yearly, multiple-day, small-group yoga retreats in pristine locations (including the Italian countryside) that combine the opportunity for sharing leisurely walks, strenuous hikes, swimming, bicycling, nutritious meals, meditation, camaraderie, introspection, and discussion. These more intense yoga experiences promote her daily classes, and vice versa, with some return students registering a year in advance to ensure they do not miss out.

In response to the reemerging popularity of aerobics such as zumba, belly fit, belly swing, and boot camps, Crompton combines a half hour of low-impact cardio into her yoga classes along with weights to compliment strength and flexibility training. Spin combined with yoga is another popular option offered by some.

With the predominance of an aging population, there is an untapped market in physically fit 50- to 60-plus-year-old clients committed to staying healthy and feeling youthful who need professional trainers cognizant of aging-related physical challenges to devise and facilitate a graceful transition to fitness practices and strategies that minimize the risk of injury. Crompton's restorative yoga, for example, offers clients a more passive practice tailored to nurture healing through soothing poses, facilitated by blankets, blocks, and other props that take into account one's unique body and sensitivities.

Wellness Coaching

Professional coaching has existed for 20 years, and until recently coaches concentrated on life, corporate, and executive coaching. But now health and wellness coach training programs are appearing, and some personal trainers are beginning to transition their business into coaching. Wellcoaches—an organization that has been a leader in the field and is affiliated with the American College of Sports Medicine—points out that "professional coaches have long been recognized for their skills in helping athletes, sports teams, and executives perform at their best. Now, professional wellness coaches are helping change the lives of people seeking lasting improvement in their health and well-being."

Playing a Different Role

As a personal trainer, you typically act as the expert, telling your client what to do and how to do it. But a coach plays a different role. Through thoughtful questioning and dialogue, a coach helps to guide the client in finding answers for herself and gain the self-confidence necessary to succeed in adopting a healthy lifestyle.

An important part of coaching is something known as the "stages of change," a concept developed by behavioral experts in helping people to quit smoking. This model reveals that we progress through a series of steps as we incorporate a new behavior into our lives.

These stages of change are: pre-contemplation, contemplation, preparation, action, and maintenance (see sidebar on page 95). For any given behavior change, we are in one of these stages. Interestingly, the basics of how people change seem to be similar across cultures in different parts of the world. In fact, Wellcoaches, which certifies health professionals to coach clients in the areas of diet, fitness, stress, and overall health, incorporates these stages of change in working with clients.

Making the Connection

Coaching can help people overcome one of the main reasons diets often don't work—the person hasn't "yet connected their heart and their head," says Ellen Goldman, a longtime personal trainer who has started a coaching practice. "They logically know that they need to lose weight," she explains, "but they haven't connected with the deep down emotion of really why it makes a difference to them." The coaching process helps people do this, so that they build confidence and a foundation to work on.

A few of the trainers we interviewed made a strong connection between spirituality and taking care of their bodies. The chain of thought on this seems to be that by nurturing the physical self, mental benefits are created, which beget emotional health, and finally the spiritual is realized. Some trainers bring religious beliefs into the equation by their belief that polishing their "gift" of a body to high levels, they honor with gratitude that which has been given to them by a higher power. By being on

Ch-Ch-Ch-Changes

Here's a rundown of the five stages of change—you'll probably recognize your clients in these descriptions.

1. *Pre-contemplation.* In this stage, the person is not even yet thinking of changing a particular behavior. They're either saying "I won't" or "I can't" do this.

2. *Contemplation.* In the contemplation stage, a person is giving serious consideration to changing a behavior—they may contact you to inquire about your services, for example. But contemplation is not commitment—a person could spend years in this stage without progressing. In fact, two-thirds of the population may be in the contemplation stage when it comes to behavior change.

3. *Preparation.* Now a person is ready to take action within the next month, although he still has yet to make a firm commitment. As a coach, you'll help him discover his underlying motivations and obstacles, and strategies to overcome them. The client will develop a health and fitness vision statement, which is a general assertion about where they would like to be in six or more months, and why. For example, a vision statement could be: "To exercise regularly and get my stress level under control in the next six months so that I'll be able to enjoy good health when I retire in five years."

4. *Action.* As your client begins to implement her plan to achieve her vision, she is in the action stage. Action is not the same as permanent change, and it's typical that a client can experience a relapse.

5. *Maintenance.* In this last stage of change, the new behavior has become habit, but the client must work to sustain the change. He risks boredom, so it's important to keep his health and fitness routine engaging and fresh.

▲

Stat Fact

According to Gold's Gym and Health.com's 2010 fitness census, since the year 2000, the amount of fat the average American consumes has increased by 180 grams (two sticks of butter) per week. That's 20 pounds of fat per year. The number of gastric bypass and other bariatric surgeries shot up nearly 600 percent, with 220,000 procedures done in 2008 to the tune of $5.7 billion.

the inside track as a professional and already fit, you may want to do some reading on the other areas of human enlightenment, in all its forms, so that you can help your clients bridge the mental, social, and emotional challenges they face with changing their bodies.

A Business for Anywhere

Ellen Goldman has been a personal trainer for years, but was intrigued by the psychological impact coaching could have on struggling clients. "When I became introduced to coaching and started looking at the psychology of behavior change, I began to see tools that would help people make significant change," she says. "I'm slowly building the coaching practice with the hopes over the next few years of transitioning more hours into coaching and fewer hours into training."

Goldman likes the flexibility of coaching, which can be done over the phone (Wellcoaches has a web-based platform allowing coaches to interact with clients). She's based in New Jersey, but has clients who live in California and New York, and she has worked with clients from Colorado and Illinois. "I love the idea of having a business I can have anywhere," she says.

The Coaching Session

The length and frequency of coaching sessions varies. Typically, the initial session is about 90 minutes, where the client establishes her underlying motivations and a vision statement. She also will figure out what her greatest obstacles will be, and some strategies for getting around them, as well as three-month and weekly goals. Follow-up sessions can be anywhere from 30 to 60 minutes. Most coaches charge at a rate similar to that of their personal training sessions.

The Challenges of Coaching

Coaching isn't something you become good at quickly. Becoming a high-quality coach takes months or even years of training and practice. In fact, "learning and growth for coaches never stops, just as for clients—it is a lifelong journey," according to Wellcoaches.

With the profession being so new, many people don't know what coaching is, so marketing is an important aspect of a successful coaching practice. "Some trainers are jumping on the bandwagon thinking this is an easy way to bring in another income source," Goldman says. "They're going to find that it's not so easy, because you're trying to sell a product that people don't understand and they can't see." At the same time, because the field is young, you can become a pioneer and get in on the ground floor. In fact, there is a parallel between coaching and the early days of personal training when the general public still needed to become familiar with the service. "Now everybody would like to be working with a personal trainer," Goldman says. "I see wellness coaching following a very similar route."

> **Bright Idea**
>
> As with personal training, there is a limiting factor with coaching in that your income depends on the number of hours you're willing to work. In order to address this limitation, a coach could work with small groups—working with five or six people who have a like-minded goal, such as weight loss, stress management, or managing diabetes.

In order to get the word out, Goldman has approached friends who are health-care providers about placing brochures in their businesses. "I'm finding that [in] my community, I'm kind of rewriting who I am, because people know me as a personal trainer," she says. "I have to get out there and say I have a new service that I'm offering."

What You'll Need to Do

Certification organizations for wellness coaching likely will become more and more prevalent—so carefully check out any particular organization before signing up. Wellcoaches is affiliated with the well-established American College of Sports Medicine, and offers a comprehensive 13-week training program leading to certification.

Functional Training

Traditional bodybuilding exercises have focused on increasing muscle size by isolating particular parts of the body. They don't typically challenge a person's ability to coordinate or balance. The bench press, for example, is done lying down, and generally isolates the chest, arms, and front deltoids, while eliminating the need to balance on the feet while doing the exercise.

But your clients, of course, don't live in the gym—everyday life involves more than isolated movements. Instead, muscles, ligaments, bones, joints, and the nervous system interact to allow a person to perform complex actions. Together these elements make up a "kinetic chain" that makes intricate movement possible.

▲

Inspire Yourself

The trainers we interviewed who were known for their signature styles all have something in common: research. They expose themselves to new ways of thinking, alternative approaches, and the many disciplines that are connected to training the physical body. Through this study they extract new context for their methods and afford more daring. They agreed that their reading lists, web surfing, and sources of inspiration change rapidly, offering quick ten-minute chunks of research opportunities here and there between other tasks.

Here are some of the books Gunnar Peterson currently has at home for sampling and inspiration:

❍ *Timeless Secrets of Health and Rejuvenation* by Andreas Moritz

❍ *Heal Your Knees* by Klapper and Huey

❍ *The Click Diet* by Scott Penn

❍ *Thrive* by Brendan Brazier

❍ *Anatomy of Strength Training* by Pat Manocchia

❍ *Anabolic Primer* by Gerard Thorne

So whether they're hoisting groceries out of the car or playing a pickup game of basketball, your clients will need good coordination, balance, and flexibility. Therefore, developing bigger muscles is only one aspect of becoming fit. What we're talking about here is functional strength, which allows the various parts of the body to work synergistically to make movements fluid, efficient, and less injury prone.

At the Core

A concept related to functional strength is core strength. In addition to your abdominal muscles, the core consists of the spine, hip, and pelvic muscles. It encompasses deeper-level muscles that help to stabilize the body and provide a foundation for movement.

A weak core can lead to injury, including lower back problems, and reduces the strength of the arms and legs. In fact, in the elderly there is a link between a strong core and balance.

Boning Up

While clients know that lifting weights will impact their muscles, many are unaware of the effect resistance training has on bones. In a study at the University of Arizona, women aged 28 to 39 performed resistance training for a year and a half. They saw increases of two percent in bone mineral density at the hip and lumbar spine. This is good to know—women represent 80 percent of the 10 million Americans with osteoporosis.

It's no surprise then, that functional, core, and balance training continue to grow in popularity. In fact, the American Council on Exercise (ACE) listed core training as the number seven trend forecasted for growth in 2012. Related exercise programming and equipment—for example, foam rollers, wobble boards, and Bosu balls—are "among the fastest growing and most popular exercise options," says ACE. So it's likely that your competitors are offering programs and classes with this type of training for a wide variety of clients. You should strongly consider doing the same if a client is an appropriate fit for this type of exercise.

The National Academy of Sports Medicine (NASM), a certification organization, has been a leader in functional training. In fact, their Overhead Squat Assessment gives you an easy and quick way to determine your client's functional strength and flexibility by viewing certain "checkpoints" during the movement. As the client squats with arms overhead, the feet, knees, lower back, shoulders, and head should maintain proper alignment. If they become out of line, this indicates muscle tightness or weakness around a particular joint. Through NASM's protocol, you can then program particular corrective exercises to address the imbalances.

Choosing a Niche

The big chain gyms target a wide range of clients—they spread their marketing net far and wide in an effort to generate business. As a smaller operator, you can set yourself apart from the big guys, as well as other small training businesses, by taking a different approach. You can target a niche market by focusing on a certain clientele—for example, athletes, adolescents, the elderly, or the pre- or post-natal population. Lynne Wells, for example, teaches a post-partum dance class for moms and babies

▲

called "Sling Your Baby Dance." By specializing, you'll gain an even greater reputation in your community as someone with trusted fitness expertise.

In fact, marketing expert Debbie LaChusa recommends finding or creating a unique selling proposition (USP) that will differentiate you and your services from other trainers and gyms in your area. "Research feasible specialties," she says. "Feasibility is a twofold proposition. First, are there enough potential customers to make a business fly? Second, can you create and/or fill a need that no one else is filling? For example, do you live in an area with a lot of stay-at-home moms? Could you cater to that audience at a central location or in their own homes? Perhaps there are a lot of retirees in your area. Could you make a business out of catering to them? Are there any mobile trainers in your area? If not, consider that as an option."

By targeting a very specific market segment, you can tailor your service package and marketing efforts to meet that segment's needs. And as word spreads of your expertise, this will attract new clients.

Consider Your Strengths and Likes

To consider the niche you would like to focus on, begin by evaluating your own strengths and abilities. Think about what attracted you to personal training as a career. Then draw a picture in your mind of the client you want to train—the person who will be satisfied with what you have to offer and whom you will enjoy spending time with.

Benefits for Growing Bodies

According to a study done by the National Association of Sports and Physical Education (NASPE), infants, toddlers, and pre-schoolers should engage in at least 60 minutes of physical activity daily and should not be sedentary for more than 60 minutes at a time except when sleeping. Physical activity among children and adolescents is important because of the related health benefits (cardio-respiratory function, blood pressure control, weight management, cognitive and emotional benefits).

Type 2 diabetes, once called "adult onset" diabetes, high blood pressure, and high cholesterol, once thought to be age-related, are now diagnosed in children and teens. See www.fitness.gov for more of this study.

Now do the necessary market research to determine if enough people in the area in which you want to work fit your profile and can afford your services. If the answer to that question is yes, you're ready to go. If it's no, then you need to adjust your services, your target market, or both.

Once you've decided what you want to do and who your clients are, you can put yourself in front of them and start building your business.

If your niche is dealing with special populations such as older adults, you need to become well-versed in the area you're addressing. Many continuing education sources offer the opportunity to do just that. The American Council on Exercise, for example, offers a homebased course called "Specialized Strength Training: Winning Workouts for Special Populations." The National Academy of Sports Medicine has a series of home-study courses for training seniors, youth, and pre-natal populations. NASM also offers advanced specializations, including the Performance Enhancement Specialist, where the curriculum includes advanced athletic training techniques.

Startup Expenses and Financing

One of the more appealing aspects of start-ing a personal training business is that it requires relatively low startup costs—unless you want to open your own studio. So what do you need in the way of cash and available credit to open your doors? It will depend on what equipment you already own, the services you want to offer, and whether you'll be homebased or working out of a commercial location. In general, homebased personal training businesses can cost as little as a few hundred dollars, or thousands. However, opening your own studio can run tens of thousands of dollars or more.

As you consider your own situation, don't pull a startup number out of the air; use your business plan to calculate how much you'll need to start your ideal operation. Then figure out how much you have. If you have all the cash you need, you're very fortunate. If you don't, you need to start playing with the numbers and deciding what you can do without, or you'll need to decide where to look for outside funds. In this chapter, we'll discuss sources of financing for your new business.

We'll also discuss the equipment you'll need to get started. Management and administration will be critical parts of your operation, and you'll need the right tools to handle these important tasks. Your office equipment needs will vary significantly depending on the size of your operation. You'll also need exercise equipment. The cost of such equipment will vary, from very little for a homebased operation to thousands of dollars' worth of sophisticated machines if you are going to open a studio. Use the information in this chapter as a guideline, but make your final decision on what to buy based on your own situation.

Sources of Startup Funds

Diana Broschka and Phil Martens initially approached Twin Cities residents who were supportive of the 1999 creation of his G-Werx machine. Those private investors liked the idea of 501F1T but told the team to prove themselves before they would invest.

Broschka and Martens continued to socialize and distribute their business plan very selectively. Though it showed deep accountability, Broschka points out that in late 2007 and early 2008, private investment dollars were hard to come by in their networks.

They turned to the banks next and US Bank was first on the list, being Martens' banking institution at the time. While US Bank saw merits in the plan and program, they did not think the team's three years of previous business operations at a starter location were indicators of future success.

Through a recommendation in their network they approached a neighborhood bank for a SBA loan and were approved with the caveat that Broschka would co-sign the loan and participate in the business. That is how Broschka, who according to the business plan was meant to be a short-term consultant, segued into a 50-percent ownership. After Broschka eventually wound up infusing $45,000 of her own money, they forged ahead, both taking less than sufficient salaries and compensation, which over time could be viewed as additional investment in the business.

Jennifer Brillian, the personal trainer in Brooklyn, works at her clients' locations and uses whatever items are at hand as training equipment, so her startup costs were nominal. She says it cost her less than $500 to register her business and have business cards and fliers printed. Even today, she owns very little in the way of equipment. If clients want or need items such as weights, mats, or aerobic equipment, they purchase those items themselves.

Bright Idea

Looking for startup cash? Consider a garage sale. You may have plenty of "stuff" you're not using and won't miss what can be sold for the cash you need to get your business off the ground.

By contrast, another trainer we talked with needed about $100,000 to open his studio; half that went for equipment, the other half for build-out. Thanks to his previous success with contracting to a health club chain, he was able to self-finance his new venture.

Most of the personal training entrepreneurs we talked with used their own savings and equipment they already owned to start their businesses. Because the startup costs are relatively low for homebased personal training businesses, you'll find traditional financing difficult to obtain. Banks and other lenders typically prefer to lend amounts much larger than you'll need and are likely to be able to qualify for.

You might want to start your business on the side, while working a part- or full-time job, so your personal living expenses are covered. But if you plan to plunge into your new business full time from the start, be sure you have enough cash on hand to cover your expenses until the revenue starts coming in. At a minimum, you should have the equivalent of three months' expenses in a savings account to tap if you need it; you'll probably sleep better if you have 6 to 12 months of expenses socked away.

As you're putting together your financial plan, consider these sources of startup funds:

- *Your own resources*. Do a thorough inventory of your assets. People generally have more assets than they immediately realize. This could include savings accounts, equity in real estate, retirement accounts, vehicles, recreation equipment, collections, and other investments. You may opt to sell assets for cash or use them as collateral for a loan. Take a look, too, at your personal line of credit; most of the equipment you'll need is available through retail stores and suppliers that accept credit cards.
- *Friends and family*. The logical next step after gathering your own resources is to approach friends and relatives who believe in you and want to help you

succeed. Be cautious with these arrangements. No matter how close you are, present yourself professionally and put everything in writing. Be sure the individuals you approach can afford to take the risk of investing in your business.

- *Clients.* If you're a successful personal trainer looking to expand your business, your clients may be potential investors, says Steve Tharrett, president of Dallas-based Club Industry Consulting (www.clubindustryconsulting.com) and a consultant to health clubs. "I know a lot of personal trainers who have clients with a high net worth," he says, "and the clients believe in them so much that they will give the trainers the financing to start up." Again, it's essential that you put everything in writing.

- *Partners.* Though most personal training businesses are owned by just one person, you may want to consider using the "strength in numbers" principle and look around for someone who wants to team up with you in your new venture. You may choose someone who has financial resources and wants to work side by side with you in the business. Or you may find someone who has money to invest but no interest in doing the actual work. Be sure to create a written partnership agreement that clearly defines your respective responsibilities and obligations. See the sample General Partnership Agreement on page 107.

- *Government programs.* Take advantage of the abundance of local, state, and federal programs designed to support small businesses in general, and health- and fitness-related programs in particular. Make your first stop the U.S. Small Business Administration; then investigate various other programs. Women, minorities, and veterans should check out niche-financing possibilities designed to help these groups get into business. The business section of your local library is a good place to begin your research.

Equipping Your Business

As tempting as it may be to fill up your office with an abundance of clever gadgets designed to make your working life easier and more fun, you're better off disciplining yourself to buy only the bare necessities. You can use the "Equipment Maintenance Record" we have provided on page 110 to keep you on track. Consider these basic items:

- *Typewriter.* You may think that most typewriters are in museums these days, but they actually remain quite useful to businesses that deal frequently with pre-printed and multipart forms (such as contracts and medical forms). A good

General Partnership Agreement

General Partnership Agreement**

_____, residing at _____
(name of partner)   (address)

_____ and _____.
                                              (name of partner)

_____, residing at _____
                                                       (address)

_____, hereinafter referred to as the

"Partners" agree as follows:

1. Type of Business.

The Partners voluntarily associate themselves together as general partners for the purpose of

conducting the general business of _____, and any other
                                          (type of business)

type of business that may from time to time be agreed on by the Partners.

2. Name of Partnership.

The name of the Partnership shall be _____
                                        (name)

_____. This name will be registered in the office of the Secre-

tary of State as the fictitious name of the Partnership.

3. Term of Partnership.

The Partnership shall commence on _____
                                   ("the execution of this Agreement" or specify date)

and shall continue until _____ or
                          (specify date or "dissolved by mutual agreement of the parties")

terminated as provided in this Agreement.

4. Place of Business.

The principal place of business of the Partnership shall be at _____,
                                                                (address)

_____, _____, _____
(city)   (county)   (state)

and any other place or places that may be mutually agreed on by the parties to this Agreement.

▲

electric typewriter can be purchased for $80 to $150. Check online at eBay and Craigslist for used versions.

- *Computer and printer.* A computer is an essential piece of equipment for any business; this is obviously so if you have a website. It also will help you handle the financial side of your business and produce marketing materials. You don't necessarily need the "latest and greatest" in computing power, but for a reasonable price you can get a desktop computer with the most current version of Windows, a Pentium processor, 1GB RAM, 160GB hard drive, a CD-ROM/DVD-ROM, and 128MB video memory. A high-speed DSL or cable connection to the internet is desirable. Expect to spend about $700 to $3,500 for your

---

Broken-In or Broken?

Should you buy all new equipment, or will used be sufficient? That depends, of course, on which equipment you're thinking about. For office furniture (desks, chairs, filing cabinets, bookshelves, etc.), you can get some great deals buying used items on Craigslist, eBay, and www.Freecycle.org. You might also be able to save a significant amount of money buying certain office equipment (such as your copier, phone system, and fax machine) used rather than new. However, for high-tech items such as your computer, you'll probably be better off buying new. Don't try to run your company with outdated technology.

Use caution when buying used exercise equipment. You may get some good deals, but you need to be sure the equipment is in good condition and safe. If you don't have the knowledge to evaluate the equipment, find someone who does before you buy used.

The Amazon marketplace positions so many vendors to compete with one another that it's a snap to find low prices on exercise equipment and office needs (even software). It's also easy to compare the features of many products. To choose the right vendor to purchase from, look for ones that have received five-star ratings from as many buyers as possible.

To find good used equipment, you'll need to shop around. Certainly check out used office furniture and equipment dealers. Also check the classified section of your local paper under items for sale, as well as notices of bankrupt companies and companies that are going out of business for various reasons and need to liquidate.

---

computer and an additional $125 to $1,000 for a printer. Consider a Mac iBook for your social media "production" needs. They start at $800 new, but you can find them used on Amazon for around $200 from quality vendors with five-star ratings. They come with movie, slideshow, and photo editing, and even soundtrack software to make you look polished on the web.

- *Software*. Think of software as your computer's brains, the instructions that tell your computer how to accomplish the functions you need. There are many programs on the market that will handle your accounting, customer information management, and other administrative requirements.

> ### Dollar Stretcher
>
> Freecycle (www.freecycle.org) is a community with a mission to keep usable goods out of landfills and has many free office goods posted for the taking.
>
> Craigslist (www.craigslist.org) has a free section that in major cities is chock full of free goods, like printers, fax machines, office furniture, and anything else you can imagine. It just takes a little patience and hunting to get what you want.

Most personal trainers can run their companies with a word processing program (such as Microsoft Word or Corel WordPerfect, which cost in the range of $85 to $400 depending on the version you get); an accounting program (such as Intuit QuickBooks or Peachtree Accounting, which run about $80 to $200); and either a general customer contact management package or a client management package designed for personal trainers, which typically cost $200 to $900. Software can be a significant investment, so do a careful analysis of your needs and then study the market and examine a variety of products before making a final decision.

One of the ways Martens and Broschka spent invested money was on fitness studio member management software, which they purchased before even opening their doors. Broschka says, "We could've selected a host of software applications across a spectrum of costs but decided to go with the more expensive software from an industry leader (www.motionsoft.net) knowing it was more than we needed but that we would grow into it. I am a software, data, and management process professional so I understand and invest in the value of systems and tools to effectively and efficiently manage our operations."

Always seeing the potential to nurture a relationship, Broschka adds, "We hope to soon be featured on their website as one of their gym clients."

Most new computers come with basic business software already loaded. If you're running a one-person operation, that may be all you need. But if you

▲

Equipment Maintenance Record

Exercise equipment needs daily and weekly maintenance to function properly and safely. Temperature, humidity, usage, ventilation, and friction can cause wear on equipment. See the manufacturer's guidelines for information on necessary internal and external maintenance. Set up schedules and keep logs to document the maintenance that's been done. Check barbells and dumbbells weekly, and tighten or lubricate as needed.

Equipment Maintenance Record

Date: _____

Equipment: _____

Work performed:

❑ Adjusted   ❑ Patched   ❑ Lubricated

❑ Cleaned   ❑ Repaired   ❑ Replaced part # _____

Notes: _____

_____

_____

Signature: _____

want to grow your company, you should take a look at industry-specific software packages designed especially for personal trainers, such as those from Aspen Software or BSDI discussed in Chapter 5.

- *Photocopier.* The photocopier is a fixture of the modern office, and you'll use one to give clients copies of their records. You can get a basic, no-frills personal copier for less than $400 in just about any office supply store. More elaborate models increase proportionately in price. If you anticipate a heavy volume of photocopying, consider leasing.

- *Fax machine*. Fax capability has become another must in modern offices. You can either add a fax card to your computer or buy a stand-alone machine. If you use your computer, it must be on to send or receive faxes, and the transmission may interrupt other work. For most businesses, a stand-alone machine on a dedicated telephone line is a wise investment. Expect to pay $80 to $170 for a plain-paper fax machine or $180 to $800 for a multifunction device (fax/copier/printer/scanner).

- *Credit card processing equipment*. Credit and debit card service providers are widely available, so shop around to understand the service options, fees,

> **Bright Idea**
>
> The Max OS X comes with easy-to-use movie (iMovie) and soundtrack making software (GarageBand) that you can use to throw sharp presentations together for showcasing vendors to clients, appealing to audiences in social media forums, and creating content for your website and blog. A recent check at BestBuy online showed it on sale for $899. It has enough storage to handle your accounting and spreadsheet software and prompts you to connect to whatever wifi signal you are closest to by name.

and equipment costs. Expect to pay about $200 for a "swipe" machine that reads the magnetic strip on cards. You'll also pay a transaction charge, which might be a flat rate (perhaps 20 to 30 cents) per transaction or a percentage (typically 1.6 to 3.5 percent) of the sale. Expect to pay higher transaction fees for internet sales, because the fraud risk the bank is accepting is higher than with face-to-face transactions.

Another option is the Square, a hot new point-of-sale convenience for the iPad, iPhone, or Android. It is a postage-stamp sized card reader that plugs into the audio port, and has an interesting fee arrangement. There are no contracts or monthly fees beyond the per-card swipe rate of 2.75 percent, plus $.15 cents. Check out the many additional features of Square at www.squareup.com.

- *Postage scale*. Unless all your mail is identical, a postage scale is a valuable investment. An accurate scale takes the guesswork out of postage and will quickly pay for itself. It's a good idea to weigh every piece of mail to eliminate the risk of items being returned for insufficient postage or overpaying when you're unsure of the weight. Light mailers—one to 12 articles per day—will be adequately served by inexpensive mechanical postal scales, which run about $25. If you're averaging 12 to 24 items per day, consider a digital scale, which is somewhat more expensive (generally around $40) but significantly more accurate than a mechanical unit. If you send more than 24 items per day, or use priority or expedited services frequently, invest in an electronic computing scale (for about

▲

$75), which weighs the item and then calculates the rate via the carrier of your choice, making it easy for you to make comparisons.

- *Postage meter.* Postage meters allow you to pay for postage in advance and print the exact amount on the mailing piece. Many postage meters can print in increments of one-tenth of a cent, which can add up to big savings for bulk-mail users. Meters also provide a professional image, are more convenient than stamps, and can save you money in a number of ways. Postage meters are leased, not sold, with rates starting at about $30 per month. They require a license, which is available from your local post office. Only four manufacturers are licensed by the U.S. Postal Service to manufacture and lease postage meters; your local post office can provide you with contact information.

- *Paper shredder.* A response to both a growing concern for privacy and the need to recycle and conserve space in landfills, shredders are becoming increasingly common in both homes and offices. They allow you to efficiently destroy incoming unsolicited direct mail, as well as sensitive internal documents such as old client records, before they are discarded. Shredded paper can be compacted much more tightly than paper tossed in a wastebasket, which conserves landfill space. Light-duty shredders start at about $30, and heavier-capacity shredders run $150 to $500.

Telecommunications

The ability to communicate quickly with your customers, employees, and suppliers is essential to any business. Advancing technology gives you a wide range of telecommunications options. Most telephone companies have created departments dedicated to homebased small businesses. Contact your local service provider and ask to speak with someone who can review your needs and help you put together a service and equipment package that will work for you. Specific elements to keep in mind include:

- *Telephone.* Whether you're homebased or in a commercial location, a two-line speakerphone should be adequate during the startup period. As you grow and your call volume increases, you'll add more lines. For a homebased personal trainer, your phone can cost as little as $60. If you have a studio, you'll pay $300 to $700 for a system.

  Your telephone can be a tremendous productivity tool, and most of the models on the market today are rich in features you will find useful. Such features include automatic redial, programmable memory for storing frequently called numbers, and speakerphone for hands-free use. You may also want call forwarding, which allows you to forward calls to another number when you're not in your office, and call waiting, which signals you that another call is coming in while you are on the phone. These services are typically available through your telephone company for a monthly fee.

If you're going to be spending a great deal of time on the phone, perhaps doing marketing or handling customer service, consider a headset for comfort and efficiency. A cordless phone also lets you move around freely while talking. These units vary widely in price and quality, so research them thoroughly before making a purchase.

- *Answering machine/voice mail.* Because your business phone should never go unanswered, you need some sort of reliable answering device to take calls when you can't do so yourself. Whether you buy an answering machine (expect to pay $40 to $150 for one that is suitable for a business) or use the voice-mail service provided through your telephone company (prices range from $6 to $20 per month) will depend on your personal preference, work style, and business needs.

- *Cellular phone.* Once considered a luxury, cellular phones have become standard equipment for most business owners. Most have features similar to your office phone—such as caller ID, call waiting, and voice mail—and equipment and service packages are very reasonably priced, some as low as $30.

Many high-end phones are close to free with the purchase of a two-year service agreement. You can expect to pay $200-$300 for a smartphone like a BlackBerry or Treo. iPhones and other touch phones run about $300. These will allow you to use email on your cell anywhere with wifi. Quick internet research, recording voice memos, taking photos, and even taking credit card payments are possible with the right phone.

Your costs will depend on how much you talk. Read your contract carefully and be sure you understand what you're buying.

Smartphone, by Tracphone, can be purchased at Walmart in the range of $30 to $120, depending on the bells and whistles you prefer. The monthly charge for six hours of calls to any U.S. destination is $35. This way, you've got your long distance, voice mail, texting capabilities, world time converter, and even a camera in one package, at one low price. For $45 a month you can be as chatty as you want and use unlimited minutes.

- *Pager*. A pager lets you know that someone is trying to reach you and lets you decide when to return the call. Many people use pagers in conjunction with cellular phones to conserve the cost of air time and control interruptions. Ask prospective pager suppliers if your system can be set up so you are paged whenever someone leaves a message in your voice-mail box. This service allows you to retrieve your messages immediately and eliminates having to periodically check to see if anyone has called. As with cellular phones, the pager industry is very competitive, so shop around for the best deal. Pagers are usually quite affordable, ranging from $10 to $30 per month.

- *Email*. Email has become a standard element in any company's communications package. It allows for fast, efficient, and traceable 24-hour communication. Check your messages regularly and reply to them promptly. Basic email services, using a standard modem, range from free to less than $25 per month. However, if you choose to have internet access via DSL or cable, you'll pay closer to $50 per month, with an installation fee of around $100.

- *Website design and hosting*. Fees for designing and hosting websites vary widely. Having your site independently designed can cost anywhere from $500 to $5,000 or more, depending on the features you select. Hosting through an independent service can range from $15 to $500 per month.

Office Supplies

Because what you sell is a service, you'll require very little in the way of office supplies—but what you need to keep on hand is important. You'll need to be sure to maintain an adequate stock of marketing materials, including brochures, business cards, and other sales collateral materials. Have a good supply of important forms, such as: the informed consent release, assumption of risk, and health assessment questionnaire, which you'll find examples of in Chapter 10. You'll also need to maintain an ample supply of administrative items, including checks, invoices, receipts, stationery, paper, and miscellaneous office supplies. If you're starting out as a solo operator, you should be able to have these items printed for $200 to $300; if you're starting out with a studio and employees, you'll likely need a larger quantity and the price will increase accordingly. Local stationery and office supply stores will have most or all of the miscellaneous office supplies you need. Many certifying organizations will have sample forms you can purchase or use as a guide to create your own. You'll find an "Office Supplies Checklist" on page 115 to help you organize your needs.

You'll also need basic office furniture, including a desk ($200 to $800), chair ($60 to $250), and locking file cabinets ($50 to $400). Used furniture is just as functional as new and will save you a substantial amount of money. You could get all of your office

Office Supplies

In addition to office equipment, you'll need an assortment of minor office supplies. Those items include:

- ❑ Scratch pads
- ❑ Staplers, staples, and staple removers
- ❑ Tape and dispensers
- ❑ Scissors
- ❑ "Sticky" notes in an assortment of sizes
- ❑ Paper clips
- ❑ Plain paper for your copier and printer
- ❑ Paper and other supplies for your fax machine (if you have one)
- ❑ Letter openers
- ❑ Pens, pencils, and holders
- ❑ Correction fluid (to correct typewritten or handwritten documents)
- ❑ Trash cans
- ❑ Desktop document trays

equipment for free if you had the time to shop and wait. The free section on Craigslist recently unearthed some beautiful, matching reception area chairs, rolls of new plush carpet, and oak desks in perfect condition in several cities. Start collecting now and save.

Exercise Equipment

Lynne Wells, a personal trainer in New York City, started with a few Thera-Bands™ and gradually accumulated other items, such as stability balls and balance disks. She teaches her clients not to depend on special equipment, but rather to work with what they have. "Soup cans make great weights," she says. "Chairs are good, so are pillows. I even had somebody working off a toilet seat one day." She says it's just a matter of learning how to give your clients a great workout by teaching them to use their bodies instead of equipment.

Feeling at Home

If a client asks you to help set up a home gym, keep these ideas in mind:

❍ *Determine space requirements.* Elliptical trainers typically use less floor space than treadmills. At the same time, an elliptical may require a higher ceiling. Many treadmills can be folded for storage. Adjustable dumbbells and/or resistance tubing also can save space.

❍ *Have a ball.* A stability ball is relatively inexpensive, doesn't take up much room, and allows for functional and core exercises. Plus, it adds an element of fun to workouts.

❍ *Buy more floor.* Not only does rubberized flooring offer cushioning, it also protects carpet and hardwood floors from sweat. Perform Better (at www. performbetter.com) has interlocking flooring.

❍ *Get inspired.* Hanging motivational posters or quotes on the wall can help a client get inspired and stay focused.

Commercial-grade exercise equipment can be a significant investment. For example, treadmills range from $1,800 to $7,000; elliptical machines range from $1,800 to $5,200. Stationary bicycles can run $1,000 to $3,000. Climbers go for $2,000 to $5,000. A packaged set of weights with a rack will run about $600, a set of kettle bells run about $180, and weight benches go for $200 to $600 or more. See the "Fitness Equipment Checklist" on page 117 for some typical exercise equipment you may want to invest in.

Sometimes the very thing you have trouble deciding to take an investment risk on becomes your main source of income. It's a good thing that Broschka and Martens were persistent until they got a bank to support their dreams. Broschka says, "The G-Werx Workout Program is our claim to fame. We generate more than 75 percent of our revenue from it and have sustained our business on this one program

Dollar Stretcher

Many exercise and fitness equipment and product manufacturers offer discounts to personal trainers, but few will make that fact widely known. When shopping, ask about professional discounts.

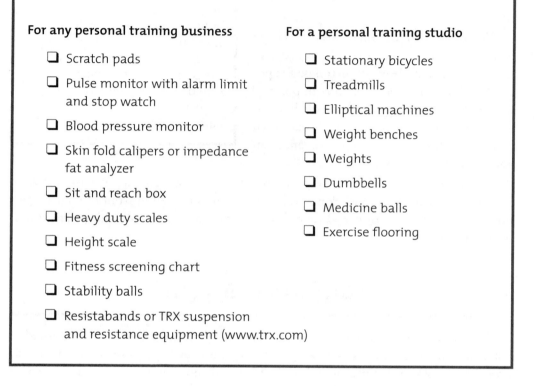

Fitness Equipment Checklist

The following checklist outlines the basic equipment you'll want to consider having for your personal training business:

For any personal training business

- ❑ Scratch pads
- ❑ Pulse monitor with alarm limit and stop watch
- ❑ Blood pressure monitor
- ❑ Skin fold calipers or impedance fat analyzer
- ❑ Sit and reach box
- ❑ Heavy duty scales
- ❑ Height scale
- ❑ Fitness screening chart
- ❑ Stability balls
- ❑ Resistabands or TRX suspension and resistance equipment (www.trx.com)

For a personal training studio

- ❑ Stationary bicycles
- ❑ Treadmills
- ❑ Elliptical machines
- ❑ Weight benches
- ❑ Weights
- ❑ Dumbbells
- ❑ Medicine balls
- ❑ Exercise flooring

through a tough economy." Broschka elaborates on the special talents that allowed this to happen: "That Phil is the inventor of G-Werx Gym, creator of G-Werx Workout Program, and Founder of 501F1T is unique in and of itself. It is rare when a fitness professional develops a machine and program, and opens their own studio."

Vehicle

If you're going to conduct training outside your own studio, you'll need reliable transportation. For most personal trainers, a small, sturdy economy car will be sufficient. If you transport equipment, it will need to be large enough to accommodate whatever you take along.

You can use your own vehicle if it is suitable, or lease or purchase one that will better meet your needs. Either way, keep good records of your automobile expenses because they are tax deductible. Depending on the type of car and driving you do, it will cost you anywhere from 30 to 50 cents per mile to operate your vehicle (that includes the cost of the vehicle, maintenance, insurance, fuel, etc.).

Keep in mind that your vehicle contributes to your overall image, so keep it neat and clean at all times. Proper mechanical maintenance is also important; it's not very impressive when you have to call a tow truck because your car broke down at a client's home, or when you're late to an appointment for the same reason.

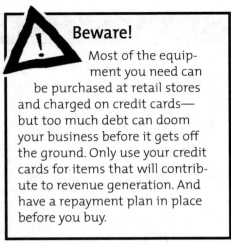

Beware!

Most of the equipment you need can be purchased at retail stores and charged on credit cards—but too much debt can doom your business before it gets off the ground. Only use your credit cards for items that will contribute to revenue generation. And have a repayment plan in place before you buy.

To promote your company, consider investing in a magnetic sign you can attach to your vehicle when you're working. When your car is parked in front of your client's house for an hour or so several times a week, that sign lets the neighbors know how to reach you.

Adding It All Up

The startup costs for two hypothetical personal training businesses are listed in "Startup Expenses" on pages 119 and 120. The low-end estimate represents a sole proprietor working from a homebased office with no employees. He has 20 to 25 clients at any given time and estimated annual revenue of $75,000. The high-end estimate represents a business whose owner has opened a 2,500-square-foot studio serving 80 to 100 clients. This owner has a staff of three trainers (one full time, two part time) and one part-time administrative assistant, and estimates annual revenue to be $360,000.

In addition to startup costs, you'll also have ongoing monthly expenses to consider. For a discussion of these operating expenses and how to keep track of your financial records, refer to Chapter 12.

Startup Expenses

Startup Expenses	Homebased	Studio
Market research (including subscriptions to trade journals and professional association dues)	$ 50	$ 75
Licenses/permits	150	150
Legal and accounting services	375	375
Startup advertising	50	1,000
Website design	0	500

Facility	Homebased	Studio
Lease (security deposit and first month)	$0	$2,000
Security system	0	1,500
Build-out (including locker rooms, showers, restrooms, exercise area)	0	45,000
Signage	0	400
Utility deposit and phone installation	90	240
Employee wages and benefits (first month)	0	10,000

Exercise Equipment	Homebased	Studio
Treadmills ($2,000 each)	$0	$8,000
Elliptical machines ($2,200 each)	0	6,600
Stationary bicycles ($1,800 each)	0	3,600
Climbers ($2,000 each)	0	4,000
Free weights and racks ($1,000 each set)	0	2,000
Weight benches ($550 each)	0	1,100

Fitness Assessment Equipment	Homebased	Studio
Pulse monitor	$129	$600
Blood pressure monitor	65	400
Calipers and fat analyzer devices	10	750

Startup Expenses, continued

Fitness Assessment Equipment	Homebased	Studio
Peak flow meter	20	135
Sit-and-reach box	116	400
Height/weight scales	25	325

Office Furnishings and Equipment	Homebased	Studio
Computer	$1,500	$3,500
Printer	250	500
Software	165	365
Desk(s)	200	800
Chair(s)	60	225
File cabinet(s)	60	175
Multifunction device (fax/copier/printer/scanner)	200	350
Telephone system	70	450
Credit card processing equipment	0	200
Forms and office supplies	200	400
(brochures, business cards, informed consent form, health assessment questionnaire, contracts, checks, invoices, receipts, stationery, paper, etc.)		
Subtotal	**$3,785**	**$96,115**
Miscellaneous (add roughly 10%)	$370	$9,600
Total Startup Expenses	**$4,155**	**$105,715**

9

Staffing
Maximizing Your
Human Resources

Successful personal training businesses can range from the small solo operator who works part time to a company with hundreds of employees. Jennifer B., the personal trainer in Brooklyn, has six teachers and trainers who work with her as independent contractors. "They work other places and do other things as well," she says. Many other trainers work alone. Whatever size of company you aspire to have, it's a good idea for you to understand the human resources aspect of owning a business.

The first step in formulating a comprehensive human resources program is to decide exactly what you want each of your employees to do. The job description doesn't have to be as formal as you might expect for a large corporation, but it needs to clearly outline the person's duties and responsibilities. It should also list any special skills or other required credentials (such as specific certifications or education requirements, or a valid driver's license and clean driving record) for someone who is going to work for your particular type of business.

Next, you need to establish a pay scale. Typically, the personal trainers you hire will get a percentage of what the client pays. Administrative staff should be paid according to the going rate in your area for those particular skills.

You'll also need a job application form. You can get a basic form at most office supply stores, or you can create your own. In any case, have your attorney review the form you'll be using for compliance with the most current employment laws.

Every prospective employee should fill out an application—even if it's someone you know, and even if they have submitted a detailed resume. A resume is not a signed, sworn statement acknowledging that you can fire them if they lie; an application is. The application will also help you verify their resume; compare the two and make sure the information is consistent.

Now you're ready to start looking for candidates.

Where to Look

Picture the ideal candidate in your mind. Is this person likely to be unemployed and reading the classified ads? It's possible, but you'll probably improve your chances for a successful hire if you are more creative in your search technique than simply writing a "help wanted" ad.

Sources for prospective employees include suppliers, former co-workers, clients, and professional associations. Put the word out among your social contacts as well—you never know who might know the perfect person for your operation. Bill Sonnemaker, who owns a facility near Atlanta, looks to

> **Bright Idea**
> Always be on the lookout for new trainers and other employees, even when you don't have a specific opening. Keep resumes and applications of qualified people on file so you have a ready resource in the event of an unexpected staffing need.

▲

It's All Relative

While hiring your friends and relatives may not always be a great idea, once you have some employees (or independent contractors) on board, you may find that their friends and relatives are a source of good candidates.

Why? Because people who currently work for you will provide better referrals than those who don't. Studies show that friends and relatives of a particular employee group will tend to possess values and performance standards similar to those of the members of that group. If you have an outstanding performer, chances are, he or she will recommend others of the same caliber.

Employees will also train and mentor their friends and relatives better than they will strangers. The relationship has already been established, and the senior employee likely has an innate desire to see the friend or relative succeed. Peer pressure is also at work in this situation. Because the reputation of the employee who made the referral is on the line, that person will probably exert substantial influence to ensure that their friend or relative achieves and exceeds your performance standards.

It's a good idea to have a policy prohibiting relatives and close friends from reporting to one another. Be careful not to allow them to be placed in situations where their integrity could be questioned, such as handling money without a disinterested party supervising them.

---

hire trainers who share his strong interest in helping and educating clients. "You want to hire people with the same vision and the same passion," he says.

Use caution if you decide to hire your friends and relatives—many personal relationships are not strong enough to survive an employee-employer situation. Small-business owners in all industries tell of nightmarish experiences when a friend or relative refused to accept direction or in other ways abused a personal relationship in the course of business.

The key to success as an employer is making it clear from the start that you are the one in charge. You don't need to act like a dictator, of course. Be diplomatic, but set the ground rules in advance and stick to them.

▲

Evaluating Applicants

When you actually begin the hiring process, don't be surprised if you're as nervous at the prospect of interviewing potential employees as they are about being interviewed. After all, they may need a job—but the future of your company is at stake.

It's a good idea to prepare your interview questions in advance. Develop open-ended questions that encourage the candidate to talk. In addition to knowing what they've done, you want to find out how they did it. Ask each candidate for a particular position on the same set of questions, and take notes as they respond so you can make an accurate assessment and comparison later.

You also need to evaluate their skills. You might ask a prospective trainer to demonstrate how they conduct a training session or how they would handle a specific scenario. And be sure to check out their credentials. Ask for proof of certification and contact the certifying agency to verify the documentation a prospective trainer provides. With literally hundreds of fitness-related certification programs offered in the United States, you need to educate yourself on the differences. See "Possible Interview Questions" below to help you start thinking about the qualities that are important to you in an employee.

Possible Interview Questions

- ○ Tell me about yourself. Or: Briefly take me through your resume.
- ○ How did you hear about the company? about the job opening?
- ○ Why are you interested in this particular position?
- ○ What companies do you compare us to?
- ○ What is an example of what you consider a "great" company?
- ○ Describe a time you had to use creativity to solve a problem.
- ○ Describe a time when you had to work in a group to overcome an obstacle.
- ○ Describe a time when you had to become the leader of a group.
- ○ Tell me about your certifications and those you plan to add to your resume.
- ○ What two or three accomplishments have given you the most satisfaction? Why?

Possible Interview Questions, continued

○ What are your long-range goals and objectives?

○ What are your short-range goals and objectives?

○ How do you plan to achieve your career goals?

○ What are the most important rewards you expect in your career?

○ What are your preferred areas within the personal trainer career field?

○ How important is it to you to be prompt?

○ Describe a situation in which you had to work with a difficult person (another student, co-worker, customer, supervisor, etc.). How did you handle the situation? Is there anything you would have done differently in hindsight?

○ What motivates you to put forth your greatest effort? Describe a situation in which you did so.

○ How do you determine or evaluate success?

○ In what ways do you think you can make a contribution to our organization?

○ Describe a contribution you have made to a project on which you worked.

○ What qualities should a successful manager possess?

○ Was there an occasion when you disagreed with a supervisor's decision or company policy? Describe how you handled the situation.

○ In what kind of work environment are you most comfortable?

○ How do you work under pressure?

○ Describe a situation in which you worked as part of a team. What role did you take on? What went well and what didn't?

○ What two or three things would be most important to you in your job?

○ What criteria are you using to evaluate the organization for which you hope to work?

○ Will you work outside in weather for boot camps?

○ Are you willing to travel?

○ Are you willing to spend at least six months as a trainee?

"Because more clubs and employers are making certification one of the requisites for employment, some individuals will try to take a short cut and forge their credentials," says Tony Ordas, formerly with the American Council on Exercise (ACE). "It's important that employers and potential clients check with the respective certification organization to confirm that the individual is in fact certified."

For administrative and clerical positions, you can administer typing and other tests that allow you to assess applicants' skills and abilities. You can either make up your own test or purchase tests through commercial testing firms or human resources consultants.

Don't accept what candidates put on their resume or application at face value; interview, test, and check credentials to be sure they have the knowledge and skills necessary to produce results for your clients.

When the interview is over, let the candidate know what to expect. Is it going to take you several weeks to interview other candidates, check references, and make a decision? Will you want the top candidates to return for a second interview? Will you call the candidate, or should they call you? This is not only a good business practice; it's also just simple common courtesy.

Always check former employers and personal references. Though many companies are very restrictive as to what information they'll verify, you may be surprised at what you can find out. Certainly you should at least confirm that the applicant told the truth about dates and positions held. Personal references are likely to give you some additional insight into the general character and personality of the candidate; this will help you decide if they'll fit into your operation.

Keep in mind that under the Immigration Reform and Control Act of 1986, you may only hire persons who may legally work in the United States, which means citizens and nationals of the United States, and aliens authorized to work in the United States. As an employer, you must verify the identity and employment eligibility of everyone you hire. During the interviewing process, let

Evaluating Certifications

How do you determine the quality of a certification agency? Legitimate agencies will be happy to provide you with information to help you make a decision about whether or not their programs are suited to your needs. Only a few organizations are accredited by the National Commission for Certifying Agencies, the accreditation body of the National Organization for Competency Assurance. Whether considering a certification for yourself or a prospective employee, here are some additional questions to ask:

○ *Is the examination nondiscriminatory?* Be sure there are no biases that would allow for an unfair advantage for any group. Ask for demographic data to support the answer.

○ *Does the agency promote ongoing education?* Certified fitness professionals need continuing education to stay on top of developments in their field. Look for agencies that require a number of Continuing Education Units (CEUs) to maintain their certification.

○ *Does the agency have a formal disciplinary policy?* Such policies are designed to protect the public by requiring the fitness professional to adhere to specific standards and policies.

○ *Who serves on the governing board?* Consider the credentials of these individuals. Ideally, at least one member of the board should be a public member—that is, a representative of the people who are being served by the certified individuals.

○ *What are the eligibility criteria?* There should be a logical and appropriate connection between what the certification requires and what the actual position requires.

the applicant know that you will be doing this. Once you have made the job offer and the person is brought on board, you must complete the Employment Eligibility Verification Form (I-9) and then retain it for at least three years, or one year after employment ends, whichever period of time is longer.

Be sure to document every step of the interview and reference-checking process. Even very small companies are finding themselves targets of employment discrimination suits; if it happens to you, good records are your best defense.

Once They're on Board

The hiring process is only the beginning of the challenge of having employees. The next thing you need to do is train them. Of course, a certified personal trainer should already know how to work with a client, but you need to take the time to teach him or her your own policies and procedures, as well as particular training philosophies you follow. Administrative staffers need to be taught your systems and have their responsibilities thoroughly explained.

Proper training in the business's approach helps instill confidence in the trainers, says facility owner Sonnemaker, who requires each of his new trainers to go through a training period of two weeks to four months, depending on the person's experience level. "If they lack confidence and they're out on the floor, the clients are going to see that and they're going to recognize the difference," he says. And because trainers come from various professional backgrounds that may reflect different exercise philosophies, a formal training period helps ensure everyone is on the same page. "It's okay that each trainer has their own personality, but the entire facility should be speaking the same message and providing the same information," Sonnemaker says.

Whether done in a formal classroom setting or on the job, effective training begins with a clear goal and a plan for reaching it. Training falls into one of three major categories: orientation, which includes explaining company policies and procedures; job skills, which focuses on how to do specific tasks; and ongoing development, which enhances the basic job skills and grooms employees for future challenges and opportunities. These tips will help you maximize your training efforts:

- *Find out how people learn best.* Delivering training is not a one-size-fits-all proposition. People absorb and process information differently, and your training method needs to be compatible with their individual preferences. Some people can read a manual, others prefer a verbal explanation, and still others need to see a demonstration.

- *Be a strong role model.* Don't expect more from your employees than you are willing to do. You're a good role model when you do things the way they should be done all the time. Don't take shortcuts you don't want

> **Smart Tip** *Tip...*
>
> Training employees and independent contractors, even those who come with impeccable credentials, to your way of doing things is extremely important. These people are representing your company, and they need to know how to maintain the image and standards you've worked hard to establish.

Get Them Involved

Ask employees for their ideas on articles, website material or newsletter content, and give them credit for it publicly! Pride is a wonderful thing and can motivate employees to confidently create more, and take on more responsibility. You can make article creation a contest by giving some examples of three-paragraph, humorous article ideas like these:

○ Metabolism with a Minimal Time Commitment

○ Put Down the Snickers, Put Your Hands on the Wheel, and Tighten Your Buns: Exercises That Fit into Your Schedule Anywhere and at Any Time

○ Yeah, Yeah. You Just Gave Birth. But Can You Do a Sit-Up? How to Quickly Get Back in Shape after Having a Baby

○ No More Dog Walks. You and Fido Need Aerobics! Fun Workouts You Can Do with Your Dog

your employees to take, or behave in any way you don't want them to behave. On the other hand, don't assume that simply doing things the right way is enough to teach others how to do things. Being a role model is not a substitute for training; it reinforces training. If you only role model but never train, employees aren't likely to get the message.

- *Look for training opportunities.* Once you get beyond basic orientation and job skills training, you need to constantly be on the lookout for opportunities to enhance the skill and performance levels of your employees. You can provide the training yourself or send them to continuing education programs.

- *Make it real.* Whenever possible, use real-life situations to train—but avoid letting clients know they've become a training experience for employees.

- *Anticipate questions.* Don't assume that employees know what to ask. In a new situation, people often don't understand enough to formulate questions. Anticipate their questions and answer them in advance.

- *Ask for feedback.* Finally, encourage employees to let you know how you're doing as a trainer. Just as you evaluate their performance, convince them that it's OK to tell you the truth. Ask them what they thought of the training and your techniques, and use that information to improve your own training skills.

Paying Your Employees

Whether trainers are employees or independent contractors, they typically get a portion of the fee the clients pay. Jennifer Brilliant says her trainers get 50 to 60 percent, although new trainers get less than that until they're up to speed. Her trainers are independent contractors, and she pays them every two weeks.

Another trainer we interviewed had a different arrangement, with trainers paid based on their revenue; the more they bill for the company, the greater their percentage. For a part-time trainer billing $3,000 a month, for example, there is a 50-50 split. For a trainer working full-time and doing well, their revenue may be $10,000 a month, and they would earn 75 percent of that. "We only take 25 percent," he says, "and the facility is still making more off that trainer than the one who is billing less and we're getting 50 percent from."

When you set a payment structure that lets your superstars make a substantial income, you accomplish two important things: You keep them working hard, because they're being rewarded, and you give them the incentive to stay with you rather than move elsewhere or open their own businesses. If the trainer is an employee

Dollar Stretcher

Rewards other than money sometimes go further in expressing gratitude for a consistent job well done. Gifts are especially nice if they are unexpected. Try giving your employees gift certificates for Massage Envy (www.massageenvy.com) An hourlong massage will set you back just $40, and having refreshed and happy employees is priceless.

and has other responsibilities in addition to working with clients, you might want to pay them a small hourly rate plus a percentage of their clients' fees.

Employee Benefits

The actual wages you pay may be only part of your employees' total compensation. While many very small companies do not offer a formal benefits program, more and more business owners have recognized that benefits—particularly medical insurance—are extremely important when it comes to attracting and retaining quality employees. Offering a benefits package makes you more attractive to prospective employees.

Typical benefits packages include group insurance (your employees may pay all or a portion of their premiums), paid holidays, and vacations. You might offer year-end bonuses based on the company's profitability. You can build employee loyalty by seeking additional benefits that may be somewhat unusual—and they don't have to cost much. For example, if you're in a retail location, talk to other storekeepers in the area to see if they're interested in providing reciprocal employee discounts. You'll not only provide your own employees with a benefit, but you may get some new customers out of the arrangement.

One type of insurance may not be optional. In most states, if you have three or more employees, you are required by law to carry workers' compensation insurance. This coverage pays medical expenses and replaces a portion of the employee's wages if he or she is injured on the job. Details and requirements vary by state; contact your state's insurance office or your own insurance agent for information so you can be sure to be in compliance.

> **Bright Idea**
>
> If you have employees, consider using a payroll service rather than trying to handle this task yourself. The service will calculate taxes; handle reporting and paying local, state, and federal payroll taxes; make deductions for savings, insurance premiums, and loan payments; and may offer other benefits to you and your employees.

Beyond tangible benefits, look for ways to provide positive working conditions. Consider flexible working hours, establish family-friendly policies, and be sure the physical environment is comfortable and designed to enhance productivity.

Employees or Independent Contractors?

An important part of the hiring process is deciding whether you want to hire employees of your own or go with independent contractors. There are advantages and disadvantages to both approaches. What's important is that you clearly understand the difference so you can avoid unnecessary and costly mistakes when it comes to tax time.

> **Beware!**
>
> Before you hire your first employee, make sure you are prepared. Have all your paperwork ready, know what you need to do in the way of tax reporting, and understand all the liabilities and responsibilities that come with having employees.

As an employer, you have greater control over employees than you do over independent contractors. Employees must comply with company policies, and with instructions and direction they receive from you or a manager. As a result, you'll be more likely to have all of the trainers in your facility deliver a common message to clients than in the case of using independent contractors. Also, you can set their hours and other conditions of employment, along with their compensation packages. Of course, you must also pay payroll taxes, workers' compensation insurance, unemployment benefits, and any other employee benefits you may decide to offer.

The IRS has established guidelines to assist you in determining the appropriate tax status of someone who is working for you. Essentially, you need to examine the relationship between the worker and the business in three primary categories: behavioral control, financial control, and the type of relationship itself.

> **Tip...**
>
> **Smart Tip**
> Before allowing independent contractors to use your facility or work with your clients, obtain proof of certification and insurance. Verify the proof by checking with the certifying agency and the insurance company.

Behavioral control means that the business has a right to direct and control how the work is done, through instructions, training, or other means. Financial control deals with issues related to the business aspects of the worker's job. This includes the extent to which the worker is reimbursed for business expenses, the extent of the worker's investment in the business, the extent to which the worker makes services available to the relevant market, how the business pays the worker, and the extent to which the worker can realize a profit or incur a loss. Finally, the type of the relationship includes written contracts describing the relationship; the extent to which the worker is available to perform services for other similar businesses; whether the business provides the worker with employee-type benefits, such as insurance, a pension plan, vacation pay, or sick pay; and the permanency of the relationship. For more information, consult your accountant or tax advisor, or see Publication 15-A, *Employer's Supplemental Tax Guide*, which is available from the IRS.

Noncompete and Confidentiality Agreements

> **⚠ Beware!**
> As unpleasant as it may be, it's important to address employment problems early—such as showing up late or not being properly prepared ahead of time to train clients. Letting these situations go unchecked can make for even more aggravation down the road.

To protect your company from an employee or independent contractor leaving you to start their own company that directly competes with you, you may want to ask everyone who comes to work for you to sign a noncompete agreement. Noncompete agreements typically consist of time, geography, and industry restrictions, and their enforceability varies by state. Have the language of your noncompete checked by an attorney familiar with employment law before you ask anyone to sign it.

Jennifer Brilliant says the noncompete that her trainers sign basically stipulates that the client belongs to the company. "It's more of a good faith thing that says 'I wish you to respect my work,'" she says.

Keep in mind that even though your employees sign noncompete agreements, they may choose to violate them. Then you have to make the decision whether or not to take the issue to court.

Building Client Relationships

Before you actually begin training a client, you need to establish the foundation of your relationship, and that begins with gathering personal data, information on their current state of health, their goals for a training program, and other details you may deem necessary. This information tells you what you need to know to develop an appropriate and effective program. Equally important, it can protect you against a claim of professional negligence. In this chapter, we'll discuss initial consultations with new clients, the necessary forms you'll need to keep on file, as well as how to maintain your client relationships once they're off the ground.

The Initial Consultation

The initial consultation will set the foundation for the relationship you will have with your client. It's a time for you both to decide if you want to work with each other. It's also your chance to show a prospective client that the value of your service far outweighs the cost of your fees.

Set up a confidential file for each client. To gather the basic contact information you should include when you set up your file, consider having your clients fill out a form similar to the "Client Information" form on page 148. You may opt to maintain much of your information in a database, and that can increase your efficiency. However, you'll still need some paper files with signatures so your clients can acknowledge that you have discussed certain aspects of their health and the training programs with them. Maintain the paper files in locked, fireproof cabinets and password-protect your electronic files.

Much of your initial consultation will involve asking questions. While you need to gather information, you should take care not to appear as though you are conducting an inquisition. Clients can often complete much of the health history information themselves (see the sample "Health History" form on pages 156–158). Then you can review the form and ask any clarifying questions that may be necessary.

The initial consultation also lets you determine if the prospective clients' goals are realistic and if you can truly help them. "I tell them honestly whether I can help them or not," says Jennifer B., the personal trainer from Brooklyn. "I'm sincere. I don't try to sell them something they're not going to be able to do." You also want to find out how the prospective client feels about exercise and fitness (see the "Exercise History and Attitude" form on pages 152–154).

When discussing a client's goals, phrase your questions in a way that establishes the value of what you're going to do for them. For example, ask things such as "How would

> **Smart Tip**
> Keep files on people who go through your initial consultation but don't sign up as clients. Put their names and contact information in a database for follow-up marketing at a later time.

Every Stripe and Shape

Be sensitive to your clients' emotions and feelings. Many people who are extremely overweight and out of shape view personal trainers with conflicting thoughts. On the one hand, they want you to be fit because that demonstrates you know what you're doing. On the other hand, they may find you intimidating because they think they can never get their own bodies into the same condition as yours. These same clients might also be very uncomfortable doing their workouts in front of others, such as in a gym or club.

One of the things Gunnar Peterson says his clients appreciate is his support. "I never tell people they're fat. I see other trainers being really hard on people and I feel like, if you're fat, you know you're fat and you don't need me to agree with you. It's like booing the home team. I want to stay positive and look forward for my clients," Peterson says.

Emotions and feelings should also be factored into your testing protocols. Personal trainer Richard Cotton recalls, "When I graduated with my master's degree, I hit the ground running with my calipers and thought that everyone needed to have their body fat tested. It took me a while to learn this, but that turns a lot of people off. Today, I can sit down with any client and give them just as good a program without testing them, just by asking the right questions. A lot of people like to be tested, and they can handle it. But for others, it can be incredibly demotivating."

losing weight affect your current lifestyle?" or "You said you wanted to fit into a size six again. Why is that important to you?"

Finally, you want to use your initial meeting to determine if your prospective client can safely embark on an exercise program. After reviewing their answers to your medical screening form, you may suggest that they see their doctor before beginning any exercise regime (see the "Medical Screening" form on page 155). A sample letter to send to a client's doctor is also included (see the "Medical Release" form on pages 149–150).

One trainer we spoke with recalls when he had to refuse to train a client because of his health. "He was a 50-year-old gentleman who smoked, was overweight, had high blood pressure and diabetes, and a history of heart problems in his family," he says. "I told him I couldn't train him at all until he had a complete physical and his doctor called me personally. He never came back." Most people don't like being told they

▲

Enrichment Provider

You and your business may be relied on for more than fitness as customers build trust and see your character and accountability partially responsible for some of the successes they begin to enjoy as their bodies transform.

Consider one of the core themes from 2009 "The Future of Fitness White Paper" as you shape the features you'll offer. The study shows that for most people exercise is a means to other goals such as health, longevity, beauty, spirituality, and perhaps most of all, sociability. Physical activity is only one of many ways to achieve those ends. Can you think of ways to compete with the gathering spots, clubs, and online social meccas people gravitate to for their social needs? Brainstorm on the following subjects to come up with ideas. Hint: An example might be a senior yoga center that holds monthly dance contests at which singles would get in shape and find companions at the same time.

Events
Online contests
Recognition

need to see their doctors, he adds, but they will usually take your advice if you are firm about it.

As the Boss

Keep in mind that when you have trainers working for you, you still have a responsibility to the clients they are training, even though you are not personally training them. Jennifer Brilliant meets with every new client before that client is assigned to a particular trainer or teacher. Then she makes a follow-up call every month to make sure everything is going well and the client is satisfied.

Pat Henry, Organic Stretching™ creator/instructor, demonstrates ways of moving that focus on strengthening the body's connective tissue and increasing range of motion.

Critical Documents

Certainly you can keep as much paper information as you want on file, but there are several documents that are absolutely essential. You should have on file an informed consent, release, and assumption of the risk form signed by the client, a physician release form, and a fitness assessment, in addition to any other critical client records.

Informed Consent, Release, and Assumption of Risk

This form states that the client is agreeing to participate in exercise testing and the training program that is developed as a result, and includes a release and assumption of the risk. You should have a client's written consent before putting them through any procedure. In general, the following elements are required for a valid form (although again, it's a good idea to have an attorney review this and other client forms):

- The person must be over 18 and otherwise legally capable of giving consent. For clients under 18, you need the signature of a parent or guardian.

- A statement that the client fully understands all the risks and benefits associated with the procedure and/or program, and a release.
- A statement that the consent is given freely and voluntarily, and not under duress or a misrepresentation of facts.

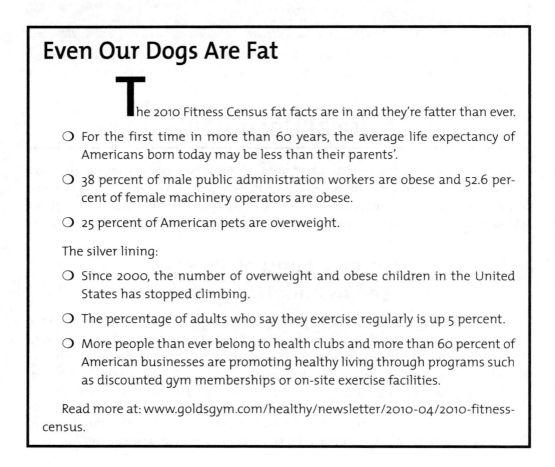

Smart Tip

Perform a regular client attitude inventory. Your clients should be comfortable with you and pleased with their program. If they're not, figure out what the issue is before you have a serious problem. A once-a-week attitude assessment will alert you to potential difficulties while they are still manageable.

Such a form should only be signed after a discussion of all the risks and benefits of a procedure or program. Give the client a chance to ask questions, and be sure you've answered all questions completely and to their satisfaction. If appropriate, make additional notes on the form to document any issues that may be raised at a later time. Give the client a copy of the signed form and keep the original in your files.

Even Our Dogs Are Fat

The 2010 Fitness Census fat facts are in and they're fatter than ever.

○ For the first time in more than 60 years, the average life expectancy of Americans born today may be less than their parents'.

○ 38 percent of male public administration workers are obese and 52.6 percent of female machinery operators are obese.

○ 25 percent of American pets are overweight.

The silver lining:

○ Since 2000, the number of overweight and obese children in the United States has stopped climbing.

○ The percentage of adults who say they exercise regularly is up 5 percent.

○ More people than ever belong to health clubs and more than 60 percent of American businesses are promoting healthy living through programs such as discounted gym memberships or on-site exercise facilities.

Read more at: www.goldsgym.com/healthy/newsletter/2010-04/2010-fitness-census.

Of her consent and release form, Brilliant says, "When I ask someone to read it, I say, 'You're in charge of what feels right and doesn't feel right. If something doesn't feel right, we don't have to push through it. We'll figure out something else.' I invite them to be in charge of making choices for themselves. I also tell them that I have lots of ideas, and if one doesn't work, we'll find some other way to achieve the results they want."

See the "Informed Consent" form that we've included on page 159. You may also want your clients to sign a general "Client Release" form, such as the one provided on page 151.

Physician Consent/Clearance

You should insist on medical clearance for any client considered high risk, and in some cases, for clients who are considered moderate risk. You can assess risk levels by reviewing their health history, medical screening, and exercise history forms. If you feel a physician's clearance is necessary for a particular client, you should request it—and it should be reviewed and updated periodically. Again, see the "Medical Release" form on pages 149–150.

> **Tip...**
>
> **Smart Tip**
> Be careful not to talk about yourself too much. Certainly your clients will want to get to know you personally, but too much ego can destroy your relationships. Focus on your clients; ask how they're doing, and listen to their answers.

Fitness Assessment

No one should begin an exercise program without first being sure they are physically able to participate in the program without injury or harm. It would be foolhardy of a personal trainer to allow any client to begin exercising without first doing a fitness assessment and health screening.

By screening your clients using forms such as those in this chapter, you'll be able to determine if they can safely embark on an exercise program. You'll also be able to determine their current level of fitness as well as their goals, which will help you to develop an appropriate program. The initial assessment should be repeated periodically as a monitoring and progress tool, as well as a way to motivate your clients.

Client Records

In addition to the critical documents we've discussed, you'll need to maintain a wide range of important information on each client. You can do this with paper records or enter the information into an electronic database. You should maintain detailed documentation on all actions, observations, program prescriptions, and discussions

▲

with clients. Be sure to record any special instructions given to clients, any warnings or limitations conveyed, progress notes, details of instruction (and instances in which you had to do repeat instruction) of techniques, equipment use or other concerns, and information on any injuries, including details of first aid that had to be administered as a result of an injury.

Keeping Your Clients Motivated

If you're going to maintain a solid roster of clients, you'll need to provide them with something they can't get by exercising on their own—motivation and encouragement. One of the most important services you as a personal trainer can provide is to help your clients stay motivated. In addition to exercise instruction, people who turn to personal trainers also need encouragement. Clients who are motivated will stay with their programs—and with you—longer.

Phil Martens uses down-to-earth language intelligently to talk to his clients. He sees some trainers making fundamental mistakes, not being very technically sound, and he says that could cause injury to people. "There are certain training methods people teach across the board that are not good for everyone. What might be good for a high school athlete may be dangerous for a senior citizen," Martens says, and advises trainers to take a close assessment, keep checking in through the duration of your relationship, and find out what clients want from the program.

People come into his gym with a gift certificate and are concerned about working out again because they have bad memories of the last time they did. "Most people don't want to die in agony the first time they train," Martens says, and suggests that the motivation levels for each client are unique. "One person wants to just get healthier and have more energy and the next person wants their butt kicked. Everyone is different."

Some of the ways you can help keep your clients on track include:

- *Listening*. Listen actively and effectively to what your clients are saying—and not saying. Be alert for verbal clues that will help you identify unspoken agendas.

- *Understanding their motivation style*. After a few sessions with a client, you

> **Tip...**
>
> **Smart Tip**
> Maintain contact with your clients outside their regular training sessions. Send birthday cards, cards at various holidays, or "attaboy" cards when they've reached a certain goal. Clip articles that you think may be of interest. Let them know they are important to you as individuals, not just as a source of income.

should have a sense of whether that person is extrinsic (that is, they need you to assist with developing strategies that will keep them motivated) or intrinsic (self-motivated).

- *Demonstrating empathy and compassion, and providing positive reinforcement.* Many of your clients won't have much in the way of a support network and may feel like they are fighting their health and fitness battle alone. Let them know you understand and are pulling for them. When they make a behavioral change—even though it may not be as significant as it ultimately needs to be—be supportive.

- *Using humor.* A significant number of your clients exercise not because they enjoy it, but because they know they need to do it for various reasons. Adding appropriate, tasteful humor to a workout helps the time pass more quickly and makes the session more enjoyable.

- *Being flexible and creative.* Clients will become bored with the same routine, so change their programs regularly to keep them interested.

- *Educating yourself and your clients.* While you may have extensive professional training, chances are most of your clients know little more about fitness than what they read, see, and hear through the popular media. Pay attention to news reports, do some additional research to get the real facts, and discuss these issues with your clients during your sessions. And realize that teaching your clients why proper exercise technique is important will help them achieve long-term success. "I would never want to have a client for several years knowing that I was able to help them accomplish their goals," says New York trainer Mike Hood, "and then have them go out on their own . . . and fail. They need to be able to ultimately take what you taught them and apply it to everyday life."

- *Measuring and tracking progress.* Create progress charts so your clients can see at a glance how they're doing. It's also a good idea to do periodic assessments, which can help you decide on what changes might be needed and also allows clients to see their progress. The best motivator in the world is a program that works.

- *Helping remove barriers.* Your clients are coping with a wide range of mental and physical barriers to exercise. Help them identify these barriers, then come up with strategies to remove them. By becoming trained in the principles of wellness coaching, as described in Chapter 7, you'll improve your ability to do this.

Clients as Allies

Your clients can help you reach your goals. If they believe in you, they may invest in your business. Make sure to make your mission clear verbally and on all of your social media channels and update your progress frequently. Two of our trainers said that clients invested in their businesses monetarily and by bartering services. Had it not been for that extra help, they may not have sustained some of the challenges of the economy.

Can Clients Reach You?

Voice mail is one of the most popular modern business conveniences and can be a significant communication tool. Even so, whenever possible, answer your phone yourself—and insist that your staffers do likewise. Handle calls as quickly and efficiently as possible. When clients call with a question or concern about their health or fitness

Salvador Mascarenas Ruiz, a certified personal trainer in Puerto Vallarta, Mexico, works one-on-one with client Maribel Quintero, pressing down on her knee to provide extra resistance during her exercise regimen.

Closely observing his client's workout in the mirrored classroom of Puerto Vallarta's Fit Club, personal trainer Salvador Mascarenas Ruiz challenges client Maribel Quintero to go the extra distance and lift her knee high enough to meet his hand.

program, they want to speak to a person, not a recording device.

Some other things to keep in mind:

- If you use an automated answering system, be sure to tell callers how to reach a live person. Ideally, that

Bright Idea

Periodically call your voice mail to see how it sounds. Make sure what your clients hear is clear and professional.

information should come very early in your announcement. For example, your greeting might sound something like this:

"Thank you for calling Personal Training Specialists. If you know the extension of the person you are calling, you may enter it now. To reach an operator, dial 0 at any time during this message. If you are a current client and need to speak to someone, press 1. To schedule a tour of our facility, press 2. For

▲

Etiquette Essentials

From a client's perspective, your demeanor says a lot about how dedicated you are to their success. So it's essential that you practice proper etiquette to make your clients feel appreciated—and eager to work with you.

○ *With a new client, ask their permission before making physical contact,* and always avoid certain body areas, such as the pelvis. As you gain experience with the person, you won't always need to ask because the appropriate barrier will become clear.

○ *Stay friendly but professional.* Dating clients should be out, as should be socializing except in a business context. A client who is the trainer's friend may tend to no longer work as hard because they think their trainer/friend won't hold them accountable.

○ *Don't socialize with others while training, and don't listen to your iPod* (yes, we've heard a story of a trainer listening to tunes while with a client). Don't eat or drink during a session, other than water. If your clients do see you eat, make it healthy—remember, you're a role model.

○ *Only take cell phone calls if it's an emergency.* If you do take a call, first ask your client if it's OK.

○ *Don't sit.* Not only is it more difficult to check your client's form while you're in a seated position, it sends a message to your client that you're not excited to be training them.

○ *If you use humor as a relationship-building strategy, avoid political, racial, or sexist jokes or comments.* Inappropriate or offensive humor can quickly destroy a relationship you have taken a long time to build.

information on our hours and location, press 3. For accounting, press 4. For a staff directory, press 5."

• Whether you're a one-person show or you have a sizable staff, change your individual voice-mail announcements daily. Callers need to know whether you're in the office or out, and whether they're likely to hear back from you in five minutes or five hours. Avoid saying the obvious, "I'm either away from my desk or out of the office"—well, of course! If you were at your desk, you'd be answering your phone. Always let callers know how to reach a live person when you're not available. Here's a sample individual voice-mail announcement for when you're in the office:

> "You have reached the voice-mail box for Jane Smith, and it's Monday, June 1. I'm in the studio today but unavailable at the moment. Leave your name, number, and the reason for your call, and I'll get back to you within an hour. If you need to speak with someone immediately, press 0 and ask the operator to connect you with Bob White."

If you're going to be out most of the day working with clients, try something like this:

> "This is the voice-mail box for Mike Green. It's Wednesday, January 23. I'm scheduled to be out of the office from 9 A.M. until 3:30 P.M. with clients, then I'll be in until 6 P.M. I'll be checking messages throughout the day, so leave your name, number, and the reason for your call, and I'll get back to you as soon as possible. If you need to speak with someone immediately, press 0 and ask the operator to connect you with Susan Gibson."

Of course, if you're a solo operator, you can't include an alternate contact, so just ask callers to leave a message.

Client Information

Name: _____ Date: _____

Address: _____

Phone (day): _____ (evening): _____

Age: _____ Birth date: _____ Gender: ❏ Male ❏ Female

Occupation: _____

Employer: _____

Emergency contact: _____ Relationship: _____

Address: _____

Phone (day): _____ (evening): _____

Primary care physician: _____

Phone: _____

How did you hear about us? _____

_____

Medical Release

Date: _____

_____
[insert physician name]

_____
[insert physician address]

Dear Doctor:

Your patient, _____, wishes to begin a personalized training program. The activities will include:

Exercise type: _____

Exercise frequency: _____

Exercise duration: _____

Exercise intensity: _____

If your patient is taking any medications that will affect his/her heart rate response to exercise, please indicate the details:

Type of medication: _____

Impact on heart rate response to exercise: _____

Type of medication: _____

Impact on heart rate response to exercise: _____

Type of medication: _____

Medical Release, continued

Impact on heart rate response to exercise: _____

Please describe any recommendations or restrictions that are appropriate for your patient in this exercise program: _____

_____

_____

_____

_____

_____

Please complete the information below and return this letter to me using the enclosed reply envelope. If you have any questions, feel free to call me at your convenience.

Sincerely,
[your name]
[company name]
[phone number]

Physician completes:

_____ has my approval to begin an exercise program with the recommendations or restrictions indicated above.

Signature: _____

Date: _____   Phone: _____

Client Release

I know of no physical or medical condition that either myself, or my physician, is aware of that could be aggravated by participating in an exercise program. I agree to advise [name of your company] in writing if this changes or if my physician advises me to stop, reduce, or otherwise adjust my exercise routine.

I will advise [name of your company] if I injure myself in any way while on their property or while participating in exercises under the supervision of one of their trainers.

Signature: _____

Print name: _____

Date: _____

Exercise History and Attitude

Name: _____ Date: _____

Address: _____

Phone (day): _____ (evening): _____

Age: _____ Birth date: _____ Gender: ❑ Male ❑ Female

Rate your exercise level on a scale of 1 to 10 (1 indicating sedentary, 10 indicating very strenuous) for each age range through your present age:

15–20 _____

21–30 _____

31–40 _____

41–50+ _____

Were you an athlete in high school or college? ❑ Yes ❑ No

If yes, please describe the sport and level of participation: _____

_____

_____

Do you have any negative feelings toward physical activity programs?

❑ Yes ❑ No If yes, please explain: _____

_____

Have you had a bad experience with a physical activity program? ❑ Yes ❑ No

If yes, please explain: _____

_____

Do you have any negative feelings toward fitness testing and evaluation?

❑ Yes ❑ No If yes, please explain: _____

_____

Have you had a bad experience with fitness testing and evaluation?

❑ Yes ❑ No If yes, please explain: _____

_____

Exercise History and Attitude, continued

On a scale of 1 to 10 (1 being the lowest, and 10 being the highest), rate yourself in the following areas:

Your present athletic ability: _____

Your present cardiovascular capacity: _____

Your present muscular capacity: _____

Your present flexibility capacity: _____

When you exercise, how important is competition? _____

Do you start exercise and fitness programs and then find yourself unable to stick with them? ❑ Yes ❑ No

How much time are you willing/able to devote to an exercise program?
    Minutes per day   _____
    Days per week   _____

Are you currently involved in an exercise program? ❑ Yes ❑ No
If yes, please describe: _____

_____

_____

How long have you been exercising regularly? _____

What exercise, sport, or recreational activities have you participated in?

_____

In the past 6 months: _____

_____

In the past 5 years: _____

_____

Are you able to exercise during your workday? ❑ Yes ❑ No
If yes, please describe when and what type of exercise you can do: _____

_____

_____

Exercise History and Attitude, continued

Would an exercise program benefit you professionally? ❑ Yes ❑ No

Rate your interest in the following types of exercise on a scale from 1 to 10 (1 being no interest, 10 being very high interest):

Walking	_____
Stationary biking/spinning	_____
Cycling	_____
Jogging/running	_____
Swimming	_____
Racquetball or squash	_____
Tennis	_____
Dance exercise	_____
Other aerobic activity	_____
Strength training	_____
Stretching/yoga	_____

What do you want exercise to do for you? Rate each goal on a scale of 1 to 10 (1 being the least important, 10 being the most important):

Improve cardiovascular fitness	_____
Reshape or tone my body	_____
Body-fat/weight loss	_____
Improve performance for a specific sport or activity	_____
Improve mood	_____
Improve ability to cope with stress	_____
Improve flexibility	_____
Increase strength	_____
Increase energy level	_____
Feel better physically overall	_____

Other: _____ Please explain: _____

_____

Would you like to change your current weight? ❑ Yes ❑ No

If yes, how much would you like to lose? _____ Gain? _____

Medical Screening

Name: _____ Date: _____

Address _____

City: _____ State: _____ Zip: _____

Phone (day): _____ (evening): _____

Height: _____ Weight: _____

Body mass index: _____

_____

Blood pressure: _____

_____

Lung function: _____

_____

Body composition: _____

_____

Cardiovascular condition: _____

_____

Flexibility: _____

_____

Strength: _____

_____

Health History

Name: _____ Date: _____

Address: _____

Phone (day): _____ (evening): _____

Age: _____ Birth date: _____ Gender: ❑ Male ❑ Female

Are you currently taking any medication? ❑ Yes ❑ No

Type: _____ Purpose: _____

Type: _____ Purpose: _____

Type: _____ Purpose: _____

Could any of these medications cause a reaction while exercising?
❑ Yes ❑ No If yes, please explain: _____
_____
_____

Do you have or have you ever had any of the following conditions?
If yes, please describe.

Condition			Description of Condition
Heart attack	❑ Yes	❑ No	_____
Stroke	❑ Yes	❑ No	_____
Chest pain	❑ Yes	❑ No	_____
Hypertension	❑ Yes	❑ No	_____
Cancer	❑ Yes	❑ No	_____
High cholesterol	❑ Yes	❑ No	_____
Diabetes	❑ Yes	❑ No	_____
Thyroid problems	❑ Yes	❑ No	_____
Arthritis	❑ Yes	❑ No	_____
Hernia	❑ Yes	❑ No	_____
Anemia	❑ Yes	❑ No	_____
Obesity	❑ Yes	❑ No	_____
Breathing or lung problems	❑ Yes	❑ No	_____
Other	❑ Yes	❑ No	_____

Health History, continued

Have you ever been injured in any of the following areas? If yes, please describe.

Body Area			Date and Description of Injury
Heart attack	❏ Yes	❏ No	_____
Neck	❏ Yes	❏ No	_____
Shoulders	❏ Yes	❏ No	_____
Arms/hands	❏ Yes	❏ No	_____
Abdomen	❏ Yes	❏ No	_____
Back	❏ Yes	❏ No	_____
Legs/feet	❏ Yes	❏ No	_____

Are you currently under the care of a physician for any reason?   ❏ Yes   ❏ No
If yes, please explain: _____
_____
_____

Do you know of any physical condition you have that could be aggravated by exercise or exertion?   ❏ Yes   ❏ No
If yes, please explain: _____
_____
_____
_____
_____

Do you smoke?   ❏ Yes   ❏ No   If yes, how much? _____

Does your doctor know that you are beginning a new exercise program?
❏ Yes   ❏ No

If yes, does he/she approve?   ❏ Yes   ❏ No

If no, is there a reason you have not discussed this with him/her?   ❏ Yes   ❏ No

Health History, continued

If your doctor does not approve of you beginning a new exercise program, why?

_____

If you have not discussed this with your doctor, why? _____

_____

Have you ever been advised by a health-care professional not to exercise?

❑ Yes   ❑ No   If yes, please explain: _____

_____

Do you know of any reason why you should not exercise or increase your physical activity? ❑ Yes   ❑ No

If yes, please explain: _____

_____

Describe any physical activity you do regularly:

Activity   **Frequency**

_____   _____

_____   _____

_____   _____

For Women

Are you pregnant now or have you been pregnant within the last three months?

❑ Yes   ❑ No

Have you experienced menopause or are you having symptoms of menopause?

❑ Yes   ❑ No

The information I have given on this form is, to the best of my knowledge, complete and accurate.

Signature: _____

Printed name: _____

Date: _____

Informed Consent

(For exercise testing and fitness program participation)

I, _____, voluntarily consent to engage in a fitness assessment, including exercise testing, and a personal fitness training program. I understand that the cardiovascular exercise test will involve progressive stages of increasing effort, and that at any time, I may terminate the test for any reason. I understand that during some tests I may be encouraged to work at maximum effort, and that at any time, I may terminate the test for any reason.

The reaction of the cardiovascular system to aerobic or weight-lifting activities cannot always be predicted with complete accuracy. I understand certain physical changes may occur during the exercise testing and during the personal fitness training program. Such changes include abnormal blood pressure, fainting, disorders of the heart rate, and very rare instances of heart attack or cardiac arrest. I understand that every effort will be made to minimize problems by preliminary examination and observation during testing, exercising, and any personal training.

Even though I will be observed during the testing and personal fitness training program, I understand that I am responsible for monitoring my own condition at all times during testing, exercise and the personal training program, and should any unusual symptoms occur, I will cease participation and inform the test administrator and/or my personal trainer of the symptoms. Such symptoms could include but are not necessarily limited to: nausea, difficulty in breathing, chest discomfort, and joint or muscle injury.

I also understand that an emergency protocol has been planned. In the event an emergency situation occurs, I am financially responsible for any emergency services that may be necessary.

I agree to assume all risks of the testing, exercise, and the personal training program and hereby, for myself, my heirs, personal representatives or assigns, release, indemnify, and hold harmless [insert your company name and your name] and their agents and employees from any and all health claims, suits, losses, or causes of action for damages, injury, or death, including claims for negligence, arising out of or related to my participation in the fitness assessment, exercise, or fitness training program.

▲

Informed Consent, continued

I have read the foregoing carefully, and I understand its content and these and other risks that are inherent in a fitness assessment, exercise testing, exercise ,and personal training. Any questions that may have occurred to me concerning this Informed Consent, Release, and Assumption of the Risk have been answered to my satisfaction. My participation in the fitness assessment, testing, exercise, and personal training is voluntary and I knowingly assume these risks. I sign this agreement freely and voluntarily, and not under duress or a misrepresentation of facts. If any part of this agreement is held invalid, I agree that the remainder of the agreement shall have full legal effect.

Signature: _____ Date: _____

Witness: _____ Date: _____

Advertising and Marketing

In Chapter 1, we talked about the tremendous potential market for personal trainers. With that in mind, you might think that just about everyone is a prospective client. While that could be considered technically true, the reality is that if you define your market as "everyone," you'll find it impossible to communicate effectively with anyone. You need to know where your

▲

particular prospects are, where they go, where they shop, what they read, who they associate with, what they're interested in, and what will push their buttons.

You also need to recognize that even though people may need what you have to offer, they will not automatically become your clients. At first, clients aren't going to just approach you to train them—you have to go out and get them. But once you get your business built, you'll find that as much as 80 percent of your clients will come through referrals.

We heard this over and over again from the entrepreneurs interviewed for this book. You have to really work hard to get those first few clients, then the rest start flowing in—assuming you're good, of course. So how will you go about getting those first few clients? In this chapter, we're going to discuss the basics of marketing your business, as well as the advertising approaches that worked for the entrepreneurs we interviewed.

Marketing 101

Marketing consultant Debbie LaChusa, of 10stepmarketing, says the basic principles you'll use in marketing your personal training business are the same as for just about any business. "It's not that difficult," she says. "It's knowing what information you need and where to get it. From my experience, many books and articles make it more complicated than it needs to be." The most important thing to keep in mind about marketing is to "understand that marketing is not an expense. It's not an administrative task that you have to do. It's an investment in your business," says LaChusa. And outside of training itself, it ought to be a function you enjoy. "Of all the necessary things you have to do in a business, marketing is at least a creative one, and you can have fun with it. You can try new things. And if you track them, which I recommend that everybody do, you can find out what's working and what isn't."

In early chapters, you learned how to identify your market. As you put together

Stat Fact
A study published by Pub Med conducted by the Brooks College of Health, University of North Florida, Jacksonville found that in congestive heart failure (CHF) patients, measurable results building a tolerance to exercise were found with upper-body aerobic exercise training. Normally, CHF patients train for heart health at an aerobic level using their lower bodies, but for patients who cannot use their lower extremities, upper-body workouts were found to create similar benefits, including building exercise tolerance and increased respiratory exchange ratio.

your marketing strategy, you need to further define your market, your goals, and your relationship to your clients. To do that, keep these questions in mind as you form your marketing plan:

- *Who are your potential customers?* Are they bodybuilders or middle-aged professionals who need help staying and getting in shape? Are they already fit and healthy, or are they recuperating from an injury or illness?
- *How many are there?* Knowing how many potential customers you have will help you determine if you can build a sustainable business.
- *Where are they located?* Is there a substantial market in your local area?
- *What are they doing in terms of exercise and fitness-related activities now?*
- *What can you offer that they're not getting now and how can you persuade them to do business with you?* In other words, what would be their motivation to contract with you for training, instead of doing whatever it is they're currently doing?
- *Exactly what services are you offering?*
- *How do you compare with your competitors?*
- *What kind of image do you want to project?*

The goal of your marketing plan should be to convey to prospective customers your business's existence and the quality of your service. Ideally, you should use a multifaceted approach to marketing your business.

You probably already answered most of these questions when you did your market research. Now it's time to expand on that information and use it to construct a marketing program.

Getting the Word Out

Personal trainers usually don't spend very much on advertising. In fact, advertising should be a very small part of your overall marketing strategy, but there are times when it's a worthwhile investment. The advertising media you'll want to consider include:

- Word-of-mouth
- Local TV and radio

- Notoriety through contests and event sponsorship
- Local newspapers
- Direct mail (sales letters, newsletters, fliers, brochures, etc.)

Choosing an advertising medium is particularly challenging for a small operation like a homebased personal training service or even a small studio. Typically, big-city TV, radio, and newspapers are too expensive, and magazines are expensive and cover too broad an area to be cost effective. You may find small local newspapers and

Veteran Yoga instructor Barbara Cromptons repositions student Carolyne Taylor to enhance effectiveness of her pose and posture.

community publications to be reasonably priced; you'll only know whether or not they'll be effective for you if you try them.

By far the most effective form of advertising, for Barbara Crompton, has been word-of-mouth, based on a reputation for offering a quality program. Crompton stresses the importance of developing a loyal following that creates notoriety around oneself as a person of integrity and a consistently excellent trainer devoted to the well-being of one's students.

> **Bright Idea**
>
> When you see an ad or other marketing effort being repeated over time, it's a good sign that it's working and you should consider using the same technique for your own company.

None of the trainers we asked thought a traditional Yellow Pages ad was worthwhile, since they get 80 percent or more of their clients from referrals once they're established.

When evaluating prospective advertising media, consider these factors:

- *Cost per contact.* How much will it cost to reach each prospective customer? For example, if you are buying an ad in a magazine or newspaper, divide the price by the circulation to figure the cost per contact.

- *Frequency.* How frequent should the contacts be? Is a single powerful advertisement preferable to a series of constant small reminders, or vice versa?

- *Impact.* Does the medium appeal to the appropriate senses, such as sight and hearing, in presenting design, color, or sound?

- *Selectivity.* To what degree can the message be restricted to those people who are known to be your most logical prospects?

Think through your advertising decisions carefully, and don't feel pressured to do something unless you're reasonably sure, based on your own assessment (not just the assurances of an ad salesperson), that it will work. Don't advertise in publications that aren't directed at your specific market. And don't buy the expensive four-color brochure when a two-color flier will do.

Direct Mail

Because of the ability to target well-defined geographical areas, direct mail can be an effective way to promote your personal training business. It also allows you to send a very personalized sales message. However, due to its costs, it is more appropriate for a larger personal training operation than a small, one-person business.

The best methods for direct-mail advertising of a personal training business are personal sales letters and brochures. Use a solo mailer, rather than including your information in a cooperative mailer full of supermarket coupons and the like. People don't select their personal trainer the way they choose barbecue sauce, so the less expensive co-operative mailer can cost you the professional image that you can effectively create through a solo mailer.

A sales letter will allow you to add an effective personal touch. It should be personal, written in an informal style, and selectively directed. You might also want to include a reply card that allows the prospective customer a chance to ask for more information or for you to contact them to arrange a tour of your studio if you have one.

Start your letter with something that will grab the prospect's attention. It might be a description of a special offer or the benefits of personal training. It may flatter the reader: "I know you appreciate the importance of a regular fitness routine for overall health." Another option is to tell a story: "Suzie Smith wanted to wear her mother's wedding gown, but she needed to lose weight and get in shape first."

Dollar Stretcher

Look for noncompeting service providers who are targeting the same market you are and figure out a way to do some cooperative advertising. For example, try doing a joint direct-mail campaign with a massage therapist.

Young and Old Take the Lead

The Bureau of Labor Statistics indicates in the 2008 to 2018 decade aging baby boomers, a group that increasingly is becoming concerned with staying healthy and physically fit, will be the main driver of employment growth in fitness workers.

An additional factor is the combination of a reduction in the number of physical education programs in schools with parents' growing concern about childhood obesity. This factor will increase the need for fitness workers to work with children in nonschool settings, such as health clubs.

Increasingly, parents also are hiring personal trainers for their children, and the number of weight-training gyms for children is expected to continue to grow. Health club membership among young adults has grown steadily as well, driven by concern with physical fitness and by rising incomes.

The body copy of your letter should let the prospect know the exact reason you are writing and what you have to offer. Headlines in letters can be very effective, but if you use one, it should describe the main benefit you are trying to promote. Expand on that point throughout the letter, reiterating that specific benefit as often as you can, using different descriptions so the reader will remember that benefit.

Any claims you make should be qualified by citing sources or offering endorsements. You should also include what the reader will lose if they don't respond. For example, indicate that you only have a few openings for new clients available, and they are filling up fast. Then close your letter with a repeat of the main benefit and a "call to action," which tells the reader what they should do next, whether it's to return the enclosed reply card, call for an appointment for a tour, come to an open house, or whatever.

You can buy commercial mailing lists (check your local telephone directory under "Mailing Lists"), but you're probably better off building your own mailing list through people you know and referrals.

Collateral Materials

A good investment of your marketing dollars is in the right collateral materials—that is, your business cards, stationery, and other printed promotional items. Just because you have a computer doesn't mean you can create your own marketing pieces. Most business cards designed by amateurs look like amateurs designed them. A poorly written brochure that does not effectively communicate your message is a waste of money. Newsletters can be a powerful marketing tool for personal trainers, but if yours is hard to read and understand, it's a waste of time and money.

Hire professionals to help you create top-notch collateral materials. Small agencies or freelancers are often willing to work with clients on tight budgets. You may even find a graphic designer or writer willing to work on a trade-out basis. While it's important that your marketing materials be coordinated and professional, never lose sight of the fact that your prospects will ultimately be sold by you, not by a card, brochure, ad, or flier.

The Real Gold Mine

Most of your clients are going to come from referrals or word-of-mouth advertising. When someone is happy with what you're doing for them, they're going to tell other people.

LaChusa, the marketing consultant, calls it relationship marketing. "It means creating relationships with your existing customers and using those relationships to either get more business out of them, or to get referrals for new clients or new business," she says. "It's taking really good care of the customers you have."

Smart Tip

Tip...

When passing out your business cards, always give two—one for the person to keep, and one they can pass on to someone else.

This just makes sense—when you take care of a client, not only do they physically see results, but they actually feel different. They believe in themselves, they're more confident, and they talk about you to their spouse, to their neighbors, to their friends. Also, by teaching clients and helping them to ultimately be successful on their own, you'll have spokespeople saying positive things about your business in the community. "No matter what your advertising budget is, that's the best form of advertising," Atlanta-area trainer Bill Sonnemaker says.

Of course, you can expedite this process by taking steps to stimulate referrals. Lynne Wells, the personal trainer in New York City, takes a very candid and simple approach, letting clients know when she has an opening in her schedule. "I also will put postcards out around the neighborhood where I work," she says. Or you can offer a financial incentive, such as giving clients a discount on their next month's fee if they send a referral and that person becomes a client.

Another way to encourage referrals is to give a gift certificate for a free evaluation and one or two exercise sessions to your clients for them to give to someone else. Do this around a holiday or tie it to some seasonal event to make it stand out. Give it in December with a note that you're happy to help your clients with their holiday shopping, or in the spring with a "Get Ready for Summer" theme.

Strictly Confidential

Prospective clients are increasingly likely to ask for references when they are considering hiring you. But your current clients may not want their names and contact information given out to strangers. One way to handle this is by asking current clients to call the individual who is seeking a reference, rather than the other way around. If the prospective client is in the studio, you might consider introducing him to people who are there for their training sessions. You also could obtain testimonial letters from satisfied clients that you can use as a sales and marketing tool.

Medical Referral Programs

Marketing your services to the medical community can be a challenge, but it can also be extremely lucrative. You'll likely find it difficult to get through to physicians because their office staffs typically act as gatekeepers and will try to block you from making contact. Be persistent and creative; the rewards are worth the effort.

Traditionally, the medical community has had a rather negative view of the fitness industry and is somewhat distrustful of the credibility and quality of the various certifying agencies. However, physicians and other health-care providers have begun actively endorsing fitness as a preventive measure in health care. Presenting yourself and what you have to offer in a professional, businesslike manner will go a long way toward dissolving the distrust that has existed in the past. Consider offering a few complimentary sessions to show healthcare providers what you can do.

You might try a personalized direct-mail campaign, sending letters to doctors and therapists outlining what you can do for their patients. However, unless the person receiving the letter will recognize your name or has an immediate need for your services, chances are you won't get a response. Personal visits will likely be more effective, but you'll probably find it difficult to get a face-to-face meeting just by dropping in.

Because it may be difficult to reach a doctor in his or her office, look for other ways to make contact. Participate in health fairs, make speeches to community organizations, and do volunteer work with groups where you are likely to make contact with health-care providers. If you meet a doctor at a social event, follow up later to let him know about your services. If you have a studio, consider hosting an open house so health-care providers can see what you have to offer.

Remember that medical doctors are not the only health-care professionals who are in a position to refer clients to you. LaChusa suggests researching other health-related businesses such as chiropractors, massage therapists, health-food stores, and supplement retailers as potential referral sources. In addition to chiropractors and massage therapists, one trainer we interviewed says he also networks with a sports psychologist and golf and tennis pros. He also does cross-promotions with nutrition stores and offers a discount to customers of a major HMO. "We're very selective about who we work with," he says. "You want to feel very confident that

Bright Idea

When you have a patient with health problems and you decide to contact their physician before proceeding with a training program, be sure to let that doctor know you will be happy to work with any patients who may benefit from personal training. Put him or her on your mailing list and make them a regular recipient of your marketing efforts.

they're in their professions for the right reasons and that they're qualified, so that the relationship will reflect positively on you."

When you get a referral from a healthcare provider, be sure to send an immediate thank-you note and follow up with details of the patient's progress. The more often you put your name in front of a referral source in a positive way, the more referrals you're likely to get.

Ideas for Promoting Your Business

Teaching people about the importance of fitness and proper exercise programs is part of the service you provide. It's also a great way to market your company. Speak to local groups (service clubs like Kiwanis and Rotary are always looking for guest speakers); publish your own newsletter; write articles for the local newspaper; let local print, TV, and radio journalists know you are available to speak as an expert whenever they are doing stories on fitness and exercise; participate in fitness-related charity events; or host free seminars on fitness. These types of activities position you as an expert on fitness and exercise, and put your name and company in front of hundreds and even thousands of potential clients at a very nominal cost.

The key to making education a successful marketing tool is to give people information that they aren't hearing everywhere else. Be creative with your presentation, and make it different and interesting.

LaChusa calls it "packaging your knowledge." She explains, "There's so much information out there on fitness, and people have a hard time wading through what's accurate and good, and what isn't." She recommends that you take the time to package that information in the form of a newsletter positioned as the one to sift through everything and provide your clients with facts. As we saw in Chapter 5, sending educational emails can be very effective in spreading the name and reputation of your business. The idea is to give clients more value than just the hour of training in exchange for their money.

Another angle on using education as a marketing tool is to offer a free booklet on some aspect of fitness in your ads or when you make presentations. The booklet could be something as basic as "How to Choose

> ### Bright Idea
> If you have a studio located in a building surrounded by taller buildings, remember that people are probably looking down at your roof every day. Paint your company name and logo on the roof, and periodically put out a banner with more information or special offers.

and Work with a Personal Trainer." When people call for the information, get their name, address, and phone number. After you've sent the report, call and schedule a follow-up consultation.

You could develop a workshop to present to office employees, demonstrating exercises and stretches designed for desk-bound workers. You may or may not earn a fee from the company, but the employees are potential clients.

> **Smart Tip**
>
> PR Newswire is an electronic distribution service through which you can distribute press releases that may get picked up by news sources or websites. You also can get added to their database of expert sources who are available to the media. For more information, visit www.prnewswire.com.

Is It Newsworthy?

When you have news, issue a news release to your local media outlets. If the business section of your local paper includes new business announcements, be sure yours gets in there. When you open a new facility or expand your services, issue a news release.

When something happens on a national level that relates to what you do, write up a media advisory with a local spin. Local reporters would much rather be able to interview someone in their own community. For example, let's say researchers at a university announce a new benefit to weight training. You can send a note (either fax or email) to the local paper and radio and TV stations repeating the news story and offering to answer additional questions. Your note might read something like: "Researchers at ABC University released the findings of a new study on weight training. I have seen similar results among my clients. If you would like to interview

Exercise and Depression

Studies prove that exercise alleviates depression, but what is the right level and duration to reap benefits? Many factors are under investigation including the strain, type, and length of exercise. Other variables include whether a patient will quit a program too rigorous to enjoy its benefits.

To see the hundreds of variables examined by specialists in the coupling of depression and exercise view the *New York Times* blog study here: http://well.blogs.nytimes.com/2011/08/31/prescribing-exercise-to-treat-depression.

someone local on the benefits and risks of weight training, please call me."

Give It Away

Offer free initial consultations to all prospective clients. Do a medical history, talk about the client's goals, and explain how you will work with them before you ask them to make a financial commitment to you. This is your opportunity to shine, to set yourself apart from your competition, and to prove yourself before you ask for a fee. The free consultation is like an actor's audition—and you never know what it can lead to, so give each one your very best.

Think about how your free consultation can be a bonus for someone else. For example, visit your local exercise equipment retailers and offer them a few certificates that can be redeemed for a free consultation and one exercise session. Suggest that they give the certificates as a bonus to their customers when a particular sales level is met or exceeded. For example, they might give the certificate (with a face value of $150 or $200) to anyone who spends more than $2,000 on exercise equipment. That person is likely an excellent prospect for you.

When a prospective client doesn't buy your services after the initial consultation, follow up and find out why. Make it clear that you're not pressuring them to sign up, but rather that you'd genuinely like to know why they didn't so that you can decide if you need to make some changes in your marketing approach or your service package.

> **Bright Idea**
>
> Create a simple behavior change citywide challenge (eat one huge salad and do 25 sit-ups every day for the next month), and promote it on local radio stations. Some stations read event details for free in their cities. Announce in your press kit that you'll be giving away prizes (free tutor time with you) and publishing the results on your Facebook page. You may get a magazine or two interested. Make the challenge simple, but interesting, such as asking participants to just change something simple for a month and then write to you about their experience.

Selling Your Business

To be successful as the owner of a personal training business, you're going to have to be able to sell people on your services. But don't let the word "selling" scare you. Most of the world's top sales professionals will tell you they hate "selling." What they mean is, they hate the vision of the slick, fast-talking character on the used car lot, or the door-to-door peddler who wedges a foot in the door and won't leave until you buy.

But that's not selling in the professional sense of the word.

When you sell as a personal trainer, all you're doing is convincing prospective clients that you can help them reach their fitness goals, and that you will do it professionally at a price they are willing

> **Bright Idea**
>
> Never say "no" to a customer. When they ask for something you don't provide, offer them an alternative instead.

to pay. You may be familiar with the sales training phrase "handling objections." That sounds much more frightening than it really is. In most professional sales situations, an "objection" often comes in the form of a question, and whether it's a question or a statement, it is usually a request for more information. For example, a prospective client might say something like, "I don't have a lot of time to exercise." It might sound like an objection or even a rejection, but it's really your clue to explain how efficient the program you'll design will be. Prospects rarely will say no without some sort of an explanation—an objection—that you'll have a chance to overcome.

One of the most difficult parts of a sales call is the close—that is, asking for the commitment and signing the contract—but it shouldn't be. If you've been paying attention, if you identified your prospect's needs and determined that you can satisfy them, then asking the prospect to make that final commitment should be a natural evolution of the sales call.

Be Prepared

Consumers of personal training services are becoming increasingly savvy. They're likely to have many questions for you before they make a decision to hire you, and you need to be prepared to answer those questions. Here's a sample of the type of questions you're likely to encounter:

- What are your credentials? What certifications do you hold, and where were they issued?
- What is your educational background?
- How do you keep yourself current on the latest information and news about fitness?
- Do you require clients to purchase any special equipment?
- Will you provide referrals from current and previous clients?
- Where do you conduct your training?
- What are your policies regarding missed sessions?

▲

- What are your fees and how do you collect payment?
- Do you offer a free initial consultation and perhaps one or two free sessions to determine if there is a good match with the client's personality and style?

Smart Tip Tip...

Take before and after pictures, and keep them in your clients' files so that they can see the improvements they're making. With their permission, you can use these photos as a sales tool. Authenticate the timing of the pictures by having your clients hold a copy of that day's newspaper.

Assessing Your Results

If your marketing program isn't producing the results you want, figure out why and make appropriate changes. Most of the time, the problem will likely be that you haven't defined your market clearly enough or that you are targeting people who are

Mark Your Calendar

Perhaps the most valuable tool in your marketing kit is the calendar. Plan your promotions at least three months in advance and stick to the plan. This keeps you ahead of the curve and virtually eliminates the "feast or famine" cycle of many businesses. Most businesses tend to market reactively—that is, they market when business drops off, but don't bother when it's good. Referencing your marketing calendar on a daily basis forces you to market proactively and keep your pipeline of new business prospects full.

Take advantage of seasonal promotional opportunities: Christmas, New Year's resolution, and "Shape Up for Summer" promotions are common. Certainly you can use these, but try being more creative, too. Consider a "back-to-school" deal for moms, who will have more time to work out once the kids are away at school all day. If your city has a professional sports team, offer a free session to season ticket holders, either at the beginning or end of the season. Look for lesser-known holidays honoring specific professions—Nurses' Day, for example—and target those folks.

not qualified clients. If you are not getting any responses, you need to examine your methods. If you are getting responses but they're not turning into clients, ask them why. You may need to work on your presentation, or you may find out that these people either don't need you or can't afford you. In the latter case, consider targeting a different demographic group.

Remember this: Just as you expect prospective clients to ask about your qualifications and credentials, you should also be looking for qualified clients—that is, clients who have a need for your services, coupled with the ability to pay you. This doesn't mean that you need to ask them to complete a credit application during the initial consultation. But you should be able to tell what the chances are that they can afford you when you find out what they do for a living, what their fitness goals are, and what some of their other life issues are. Whatever you do to market your business, make sure every element of your campaign reflects your overall goals and the personality of your operation.

12

Fiscal
Fitness

To be a success in the personal training business, it's not enough for you to be physically fit. Your company needs to be fiscally fit, as well. One of the key indicators of the overall health of your business is its financial status, and it's important that you monitor your financial progress closely. The only way you can do this is to keep good records. In this chapter, we'll delve into what

▲

you need to know about record-keeping and financial statements, as well as pricing your services and billing clients.

Pricing Your Services

The two primary fee structures you'll use are hourly and flat-fee contract service agreements. While some trainers use one or the other exclusively, most use a combination. It's a good idea to offer a variety of service agreements and hourly rate structures, but not so many that your prospective clients are confused. Keep your fee structures simple, but with sufficient options to suit both your clients' ability to pay and their individual fitness needs.

Finding that perfect rate that isn't too low or too high is a challenge for most personal trainers. If you're going to have a successful, profitable company, you can't price yourself too low. On the other hand, it would be equally unwise to price yourself higher than what your market is willing and able to pay.

Pricing can be tedious and time-consuming, particularly if you don't have a knack for juggling numbers. Especially in the beginning, don't rush through this process. You need to consider a number of factors.

- *Overhead.* This includes the various costs involved in operating your business, such as rent/mortgage, payroll, insurance, taxes, advertising, debt service, utilities, professional services such as accountants and attorneys, telephone, office supplies, etc.

- *Desired income.* How much do you want to be able to take out of the business? Depending on your structure, this would be either your salary or the business's net profit.

- *Capacity.* How much time can you reasonably expect to be working with clients? Another way to think of this is to figure out how many billable hours you'll have. For example, if you're working with clients in their homes, your travel time will likely not be billable, so think about how many hours you can realistically expect to be training. You'll also need to spend time doing administrative tasks; those are not hours you can bill to a client, either.

Calculate your monthly overhead. Some items, such as insurance premiums, may be paid once or twice per year, so you need to prorate those costs and factor them into your figures. Then add on your desired income or profit. Divide that by the number of billable hours you have in a month, and you have an hourly rate baseline. This number can guide what you charge when working by the hour, and serve as the basis when

---

Flex Time

Though the assumption is that a personal training session is one hour, it doesn't have to be. You could offer 30-minute sessions; you might also consider a "50-minute hour," such as counselors and massage therapists generally do.

"There was a school of thought in the '60s, popularized by Bob Gadja, that said there's a finite amount of blood in the body and you can't shunt it into one area when it's at work in another area, but if you sequence it right you can elevate your heart rate properly to an exertion that creates an amazing workout in a lot less time," Gunnar Peterson says, and advises new trainers to stay open to all types of fitness education and to read as much as possible.

---

developing contract packages. If this hourly rate is at or under the going rate in your market, you're in good shape. That will likely be the case if you're working from your home or only part time and have little overhead.

If this hourly rate is overpriced for your market, you have a few options. You can go back and look for ways to reduce your overhead or your desired income. You can look for possible supplemental income opportunities that will allow you to reduce your hourly rate while still meeting your income requirements. For example, you might consider selling a variety of health and fitness products along with training your clients. If you have a studio, you might be able to sublet or rent out a portion of your space to a related health and fitness service provider who is not in direct competition with you. Or, if you can justify the higher rate and there are enough people in your market who will pay it, market yourself based on specialized services and high quality. Take the approach of the popular cosmetics line that admits to costing more, but says its customers are worth it.

Pat Henry's ten-hour-long weekend workshops, which can accommodate up to 14 participants, run approximately $150. In Mexico, classes designed for seven to ten students are priced at 500 pesos (approximately 50 U.S. dollars) for one month of twice-weekly, hourlong sessions.

Tyrone Minor believes when people see your service rate is appropriate for the qualifications you've earned, then it is better to charge at the high end of that scale, rather than breaking your rate down into a psychologically "discounted" rate to get customers to feel they can afford you. For example, if he offers them one $100 session in which they can get the knowledge they need to quickly accomplish their goals, and he meets with them a few times, it's actually less expensive for them than a 10-session package at $50 per unit. But for some reason people tend not to understand that.

Barbara Crompton's yoga class fees encompass three different price points, structured to encourage more frequent attendance in exchange for reduced charges. Pricing varies widely between Canada and Mexico, with drop-in rates of approximately $15 and $10, respectively, and a ten-visit pass offering a 20 percent discount. An unlimited usage pass, good for a month, usually also extends an additional 20 percent savings.

Teacher compensation varies from around $18 per hour in Puerto Vallarta to $70 in Vancouver. A fitness business owner will find the financial reward is far greater in direct correlation with the costs of running the business. Having a three-to-five-million-dollar insurance policy, for example, for personal liability protection in the event of perceived negligence and additional coverage for property-related claims is not uncommon.

Within the yoga community, bartering for services is a popular means of containing costs. In exchange for training in an apprenticeship capacity, for example, a technically savvy student may "pay for" his or her experience with website design or photography skills. Likewise, hotel accommodations may be gratis for the teacher who brings a dozen or so out-of-town paying guests to the site for a workshop. Although fitness instructors in Mexico average only 75 pesos per class, Salvador Mascarenas Ruiz charges 220 pesos (still low by U.S. standards) for a 45-to-50-minute session, whether with one client or a group, because of his considerable experience.

Jennifer Brilliant, the personal trainer in Brooklyn, bases her fees in large part on how strong the market is and what other trainers are charging. She has steadily increased her fee per session over the years. "It's anywhere from $75 to $175, depending on the situation, and the clients I've had for a longer time pay less because they started a long time ago," she says. "The clients I start with now pay a higher rate."

Lynne Wells, another personal trainer in New York, started out charging the same rate as the staff trainers at the gym she used, but eventually raised her fees. Because she goes to her clients' homes and offices, she factors travel time into her rates.

Another option is to not charge by the session but rather for a monthly package with a minimum of three months, with clients paying in advance at the first of the month. Or consider offering several tiers of pricing. You can have one for one-on-one training with a long-term commitment. You might also develop several packages designed to target less affluent clients who can't afford

Bright Idea

Give yourself a raise. Every year, review your fee structures and, if appropriate, increase what you're charging. Your clients will understand if you give them sufficient notice.

to see you three times per week for several years. Those packages can be designed to help someone get started, make sure they know how to do the exercises correctly, and monitor them periodically to measure their progress and make adjustments as necessary. It's quite likely that the client who can't afford $200 per week for a year would still be willing to pay $600 for ten visits over a six-month period.

Payment Methods

An important part of your pricing policy is how clients actually pay you. For example, will they pay by the session on an as-you-go basis? Or by the month in advance? Or by the month in arrears?

Certainly, it would be ideal if everyone paid by the month in advance, but Jennifer Brilliant says, "some people are not comfortable doing that. I have people who pay at the beginning of the month for that month. I have people I invoice at the end of the month, and they pay sometime during the following month."

Something to keep in mind is that payment in advance on a monthly basis makes it easier to enforce your cancellation policy. You will want to consider how clients pay when setting your fee structure.

Accepting Credit and Debit Cards

The personal trainers we talked with were divided on the issue of accepting debit and credit cards. In general, the small one-person operations did not accept cards, and the owners did not find that to be a problem. Larger operations did accept cards, and owners found it to be an easier way of handling clients on a contract program.

It's much easier now to get merchant status than it has been in the past. Today, merchant status providers are competing aggressively for your business. To get a credit card merchant account, start with your own bank. Also check with various professional associations that offer merchant status as a member benefit. Shop around; this is a competitive industry, and it's worth taking the time to get the best deal.

Setting Credit Policies

When you extend credit to someone, you are essentially providing an interest-free loan. You wouldn't expect someone to lend you money without getting information from you about where you live and work, and your potential ability to repay. It just makes sense that you would want to get this information from someone you are lending money to. Reputable companies and individuals will not object to providing you with credit information. Be sure you have the client's full name, home and work addresses, telephone numbers, and banking information.

> **Tip...**
>
> **Smart Tip**
> Once you've established your policies on extending credit, be sure to apply them consistently. Failure to do so will confuse your clients, make them wonder about your professionalism, and leave you open to charges of discrimination.

Your credit policy should include a clear collection strategy. Do not ignore overdue bills; the older a bill gets, the less likely it will ever be paid. Be prepared to take action on past-due accounts as soon as they become past due.

Billing

If you're extending credit to your clients, you need to establish and follow sound billing procedures. Though most of your clients will be individuals, you may have occasion to bill companies for your services. Coordinate your billing system with their accounts payable procedures. Candidly ask what you can do to ensure prompt payment; that may include confirming the correct billing address and finding out what documentation may be required to help them determine the validity of the invoice. Keep in mind that many large companies pay certain types of invoices on certain days of the month.

> **Beware!**
> Mail thieves operate even in the nicest of neighborhoods. If you receive checks in the mail, rent a post office box so you know they'll be secure.

Find out if your customers do that and schedule your invoices to arrive in time for the next payment cycle.

Most computer bookkeeping software programs include basic invoices. See the sample invoice below. If you design your own invoices and statements, be sure they're clear and easy to understand. Detail each item and indicate the amount due in bold with the words "Please pay" in front of the total. A confusing invoice may get set aside for clarification, and your payment will be delayed.

Invoice

Personal Training Services of Houston

1234 Fort Worth Highway
Houston, TX 01234

Date: _____

Invoice No.: _____   P.O. No.: _____

Terms: _____

Description	**Amount**
_____	_____
_____	_____
_____	_____
_____	_____
_____	_____
_____	_____

Total _____

Please pay: $_____ **by** _____

Introduce a friend to exercise and fitness! Call today for a certificate good for a free initial consultation and free exercise session: (012) 555-0124.

Your invoice should also clearly indicate the terms under which you've extended credit. Terms include the date the invoice is due, any discount for early payment, and additional charges for late payment. For example, terms of "net 30" means the entire amount is due in 30 days; terms of "2–10, net 30" means that the customer can take a 2 percent discount if the invoice is paid in 10 days, but the full amount is due if the invoice is paid in 30 days.

It's also a good idea to specifically state the date the invoice becomes past due to avoid any possible misunderstanding. If you are going to charge a penalty for late payment, be sure your invoice states that it is a late payment or rebilling fee, not a finance charge.

Finally, use your invoice as a marketing tool. Mention any upcoming specials, new services, or other information that may encourage your customers to use more of your services. Add a flier or brochure to the envelope—even though the invoice is going to an existing client, you never know where your brochures will end up.

Keeping Records

Keeping good records helps you generate the financial statements that tell you exactly where you stand and what you need to do next. There are a number of excellent computer accounting programs on the market to help you with this task, or you can handle the process manually. You might also want to ask your accountant for assistance getting your system of books set up. The key is to do that from the very beginning, and keep your records current and accurate throughout the life of your company.

The key financial statements you need to understand and use regularly are:

- *Profit and loss statement.* This is also called the P&L or the income statement. It illustrates how much your company is making or losing over a designated period—monthly, quarterly, or annually—by subtracting expenses from revenue to arrive at a net result, which is either a profit or a loss. See the "Income Statement" on page 185 for an idea of what this financial statement looks like for two hypothetical personal training businesses.

- *Balance sheet.* This is a table showing your assets, liabilities, and capital at a specific point. A balance

> **Smart Tip**
>
> If you have to raise prices, make sure the price increase is reasonable, give your clients notice, and explain why you're doing it. You may lose some clients when you increase your prices, but generally the increased revenue will make up for it.

Income Statement

The income statement (or profit and loss statement) is a simple, straightforward report on your company's cash-generating ability. You can prepare an income statement based on your company's actual performance, or, in the case of a new company, you can prepare a projected income statement as a forecasting and planning tool. This monthly income statement depicts the two hypothetical personal training businesses used for the "Startup Expenses" in Chapter 8. One is a homebased business, with 20 to 25 clients; the other is a studio (2,500 square feet) that serves 80 to 100 clients.

	Homebased	Studio
Monthly Income	$6,250	$30,000
Monthly Expenses		
Rent	$0	$1,100
Phone/utilities	0	300
Postage	8	40
Owner/manager salary	4,000	10,000
Payroll/independent contractor commissions	0	10,000
Professional services (legal, accounting)	40	100
Advertising	0	25
Internet service provider	15	125
Office supplies	20	75
Equipment/facility maintenance	0	50
Transportation	922	185
Insurance (including professional liability, general liability, property, casualty, etc.)	50	125
Subscriptions/dues	20	75
Continuing education	50	175
Miscellaneous	100	300
Total Expenses	**$5,225**	**$22,675**
Net Profit (Pre-Tax)	**$1,025**	**$7,325**

▲

sheet is typically generated monthly, quarterly, or annually when the books are closed.

- *Cash flow statement.* This statement summarizes the operating, investing, and financing activities of your business as they relate to the inflow and outflow of cash. As with the profit and loss statement, a cash flow statement is prepared to reflect a specific accounting period, such as month, quarter, or year.

Successful business owners review these reports regularly, at least monthly, so they always know where they stand and can quickly move to correct minor difficulties before they become major financial problems. Jennifer Brilliant does her bookkeeping weekly and studies her financial statements at the same time. "It's a discipline I keep up on the weekends after the week is finished, and I can track my financial progress that way," she says.

Revisiting your plans and reassessing your goals every year or two will help you stay clear on where your investments should go. Use the "Strategic Planning Worksheet" on page 187 to figure out where you are now, and one year from now. Use it in tandem with your financial projections.

Ask Before You Need

Just about every growing business experiences economic rough spots and requires financing of some type sooner or later. Plan for the costs of growth and watch for signs

---

The Taxman Cometh

Businesses are required to pay a wide range of taxes, and there are no exceptions for personal training business owners. Keep good records so you can offset your local, state, and federal income taxes with the expenses of operating your company. If you have employees, you'll be responsible for payroll taxes. If you operate as a corporation, you'll have to pay payroll taxes for yourself; as a sole proprietor, you'll pay self-employment tax. Then there are property taxes, taxes on your equipment and inventory, fees, and taxes to maintain your corporate status, your business license fee (which is really a tax), and other lesser-known taxes. Take the time to review all of your tax liabilities with your accountant.

Strategic Planning Worksheet

Question To Be Answered	Strategic Plan Element
Where have we been?	History
Where are we now?	Context
Where should we go and why?	Vision
What is our work toward the vision? Who are we? What is our niche now to work toward the vision?	Mission
What will guide the work we choose to do and the way we do the work (e.g. inclusively, multi-disciplinarily?)	Values
What is in our way of realizing our vision?	Critical Obstacles
What will we do to reach our vision?	Strategic, Long-term Goals/Directions
What will we do in year 1, year 2...	Short-term Goals or Objectives
How will we know if we are successful?	Indicators of Success/Benchmarks
What infrastructure is needed to carry out the work in this plan?	Infrastructure Assessment
What will we do in the next three months, six months, year, year 2, year 3...	Implementation Plan
How will the plan be disseminated and to whom?	Dissemination Plan
How will we monitor the plan and assess our progress?	Monitoring and Revising Strategic Plan

of developing problems so you can figure out how to best deal with them before they turn into a major crisis.

Asking for money before you need it is especially important if you're going to be applying for a loan, whether it's from a private individual or a commercial loan source such as your bank. Most lenders are understandably reluctant to extend credit to a business in trouble. So plan your growth and presell your banker on your financial needs. Such foresight demonstrates that you are an astute business owner on top of every situation. Your chances of obtaining the funding you need will improve significantly.

13

Tales from the Trenches

By now, you should know how to get started and have a good idea of what to do—and not do—in your own personal training business. But nothing teaches like the voice of experience. So we asked owners of established personal training operations to tell us what has contributed to their success. Here's what they had to say.

Know What Your Clients Know

Beyond keeping up with your own professional education, pay attention to what your clients are learning. Reading professional journals is important, but not enough. You need to also be reading popular publications from the world of magazines, newspapers, and the internet. These are the primary sources of information for most of your clients. They are constantly reporting on new trends in fitness, exercise, and nutrition, and it's not uncommon for their credibility to be questionable. When your clients are exposed to misinformation, they will likely look to you to confirm or refute what they've learned.

Sleep Research Is Hot Right Now!

Most of the trainers we interviewed talked about the role rest and sleep play in attaining a high level of fitness. Is advising your client base to rotate muscle group workouts and get eight hours of a sleep a night enough? It's not enough, because as some of our trainers pointed out, many times those last 4 or 5 pounds that won't seem to budge are revealed to be a result of sleep deprivation.

In the beginning, clients will agree to get adequate sleep and report that they are eating in their trainers' prescribed styles. Later, trainers start to see evidence that this just isn't so. People are often not honest with themselves, thinking that if they are in bed for seven hours, this is almost as good as eight and will suffice. The truth is that they usually are not asleep the whole time, some of them bringing work into their beds, or dealing with other sleep disturbances that cause them to collect only five or six hours a night. Studies consistently show that adults need eight to nine hours, or more.

Tyrone Minor of Chizel Inc. says that the two parts of getting and staying fit are slightly different, but both involve sleep discipline. "To stay fit after you've gotten through the first and more difficult part of getting fit is not as hard," he says. "There is less training and time involved. But in the beginning you have to be so intensely disciplined with diet and sleep that a lot of people don't have what it takes to get to that goal. Sleep is extremely important and there is no way you'll see the results that you want if you don't adhere to that part of the equation. The mental energy it requires to get to your goal is vast, and if you get partway to your goal and then let yourself go a little bit, you create weight fluctuations. If you continue fluctuating it's not healthy mentally or physically."

Here are some facts you can use to impress upon your clients how essential sleep is to their success.

Sleep Thieves, an exploration into the science and mysteries of sleep by Stanley Coren, reveals a 6 percent rise in accidental deaths and 7 percent rise in traffic accidents during the first four days following spring daylight savings time shifts, when we lose an hour of sleep. Coren believes we accrue a sleep debt that can be measured by how we react to our daily activities between 1:00 P.M. and 4:00 P.M., when our biological clock winds down. Evidence of sleep debt measured in this window includes the urge to doze off during a boring lecture, and difficulty staying awake during a night drive home when the body is nearing the zone of greatest sleep pressure—1:00 A.M. and 4:00 A.M.

Coren says if a person is getting adequate sleep, they do not experience the danger of falling asleep at the wheel or inconvenience of dozing off during a lecture. Additional evidence demonstrates the challenges subjects face when solving the simplest problems while sleep deprived. Coren believes sleep so powerfully affects mental health and decision making, he shows the Exxon Valdez oil spill, shuttle Challenger disaster, and nuclear accidents at both Chernobyl and Three Mile Island all to be associated with people suffering from sleep deprivation. Tell that to your clients and see if they make more of an effort to get quality sleep!

Author Paul Martin exposes the importance of both sleeping and dreaming in *Counting Sheep: The Science and Pleasures of Sleep and Dreams*, pointing out that insomniacs on average experience more anxiety, higher metabolic rates (lest you think this a good thing, keep reading, because it's negated by the next thing on the list), a slightly higher body temperature, and higher levels of the stress hormones cortisol and adrenaline, which as you may know from recent popular news coverage, is one of the causes of weight gain when the chemicals hang around for an extended period of time in your body.

There is a level of guilt around sleeping in our current culture of immediacy and speed; people brag about their ability to get by on only five hours of sleep. Many famous people have reputations for the same, which Martin reveals to be inaccurate, proving Napoleon, Thomas Edison, and Churchill—all famous for needing little sleep—to be frequent daytime nappers, making up for sleep lost during the night. See the "Sleep Habit Tip Sheet" on page 192 and consider giving it to your clients and asking that they study it and take it seriously.

Fitness expert and TV show host of *Morning Stretch* Joanie Greggains talks about the connection between working late instead of sleeping in her book, *Fit Happens*. Greggains writes that a lack of sleep results in increased appetite from stress when the body is craving the calming, sedative effect that should be gotten with sleep, but instead manifests as a craving for carbs and sugar for those who will not or cannot sleep when their bodies want to. The carb snacking allows the body to produce serotonin, which it needs after staying awake late produces too much cortisol. The serotonin calms us after the cortisol makes us edgy. So if you don't sleep when you should, you'll eat more than you should.

With escalating health-care costs, Pat Henry sees people slowly realizing they need to be personally accountable for their own wellness. More savvy consumers in search

Sleep Habit Tip Sheet

You may want to consider making this list of sleep goals part of the working agreement you create with each client, because if they don't take these habits seriously, their health and fitness results will be lagging. This list is compiled from leaders in sleep research.

○ Invest in a wonderfully comfortable bed that you look forward to climbing into.

○ Eat a small carbohydrate snack just before turning in.

○ Exercise regularly in the early part of the day, never after 5:00 P.M.

○ Limit caffeine to one or two cups before 10:00 A.M.

○ Avoid any electronic mental stimulation before bed such as computer or phone use and watching TV.

○ Go to sleep at the same time each night and get up at the same time each morning.

○ Take a short bath before bed.

○ Use your bedroom for sleep and sex only.

○ Do not have electronics in your bedroom.

○ If you feel tired during the day, take a nap (20 to 40 minutes) without guilt.

○ Be asleep when the night sky is dark, or shortly after it turns.

○ Keep your bedroom for sleep slightly cooler than you normally would.

○ Go to bed half an hour earlier than you have been for a few weeks to start your healthy sleep habit.

○ Keep your bedroom dark and use earplugs.

---

of ways to improve their fitness will increase the need for knowledgeable, professional trainers to help in that effort.

Another eventuality that Henry hopes to see realized is the dissemination of Organic Stretching™ principles to medical practitioners. She says that currently, physicians are not thoroughly trained in connective tissue, which is the most prolific molecular structure in our bodies. It is what makes our bodies what they are, providing us with essential support. For example, in addition to stabilizing a broken limb with a cast or brace, she would love to see Organic Stretching™ applied as part of the treatment process, so the patient would learn how to move available surrounding joints and connective tissue in order to stimulate the nerves and circulation of lymph and blood to promote faster healing.

Education specialization can come from seeking work in niche areas. In addition to his formal training, experience, and disposition toward teaching, Salvador Mascarenas Ruiz's clients enjoy the benefit of on-the-job knowledge he acquired over a five-year period working at a rehabilitation clinic for Down syndrome patients. That opportunity gave him valuable insights into bone structure, strengthening one's body by working out, and avoiding injury during exercise.

Stay Flexible

We don't mean physically flexible—although certainly that's important, too—but flexible in terms of how you operate and relate to your clients. "This is such a personal business and you're dealing with people one-on-one," says Jennifer Brilliant. "Things come up and you need to remain flexible."

Lynne Wells, a personal trainer in New York City, advises that if you are bending a policy, make sure your client knows it and appreciates it. For example, if someone cancels with less than a 24-hour notice because they're sick and you decide not to charge them, make it clear by saying something like, "You know I have a 24-hour cancellation policy, and technically you should have paid for this session. But I understand that you're sick, so I'm not going to charge you this time." Now that she is a mother, she says, she is more understanding of family emergencies and the needs of children. "However, I still try to stick with the cancellation policy as much as possible," she explains. "After all, this is my income."

Assign Homework

Make your sessions last longer than the actual time you're together by giving your clients things to do between sessions. "I always give them homework," says Wells. "Usually it's just a little exercise or two to do on their own. It might even be simpler than that, like the [client] whose homework assignment was to practice standing with her feet underneath her more instead of having them wider than her hips, and to keep her toes straight instead of turned out—because that's biomechanically better for her body. It might be some basic breathing exercises. I've had [clients] do food diaries or workout journals, and then we talk through what they wrote down in a future session or by email."

Pick Up After Your Clients

Clients may be careless with their belongings, so be willing to put things like eyeglasses and watches out of harm's way. One of Wells's clients took her glasses off and put them on the floor during a session, and Lynne stepped on them. "Luckily, they didn't break," she recalls. "Now, if any client takes their glasses off, I pick them up and put them on a shelf."

Tips for Success

○ *Keep your education current.* The fitness industry is full of new information and technology. Commit yourself to constant education to maintain your effectiveness.

○ *Learn from others' mistakes and successes.* Study other personal training services and understand what they did wrong—and right—then use that information in developing your own company.

○ *Network constantly.* Always look for opportunities to let people know what you do. Consider joining professional groups that promote networking and referrals, such as a lead exchange club.

○ *Don't be afraid to charge what you're worth.* Many personal trainers make the mistake of underpricing in the beginning. When you start out too low, it's hard to get your prices up to where they should be.

○ *Pay attention to the business.* Keeping up with what's involved in running a business is challenging, and you may be tempted to let it slide in favor of doing things you enjoy more. But if you don't keep your financial and client records in order and handle the myriad of other tasks involved in running a company, your business is doomed to failure.

○ *Listen actively.* Pay attention to what your clients say—and don't say—with words and body language.

Invest in Education

Knowledge builds confidence, so invest in education—even after you've obtained your initial certifications. What the professional associations offer and require varies depending on the particular certification you have. The organization that issues your certification will let you know what you need to do to keep it current. Beyond that, you need to be reading and studying to stay up-to-date on fitness trends and news. Studying current literature, attending classes, and going to conventions and conferences are all investments in your business, not expenses.

Stat Fact

The Bureau of Labor Statistics' findings for the 2008 to 2018 decade predict people who obtain specialized additions to their fitness degrees will have better opportunities because clients prefer to work with people they perceive as higher-quality trainers. Trainers who incorporate new technology and wellness issues as part of their services may be in more demand.

You Are Not Your Client

A very minuscule percentage of your clients will think and act like you do. Don't develop exercise programs that would be effective for you; put together programs that will work for your clients. "The majority of trainers train their clients like they train themselves, and they don't really listen to the client," says one trainer we consulted. "They don't pay attention to the client's body, and quite possibly aren't doing the best for that particular client."

Maintain a Client Base

One of the most common reasons personal training businesses fail is simply the inability to establish and maintain a steady client base. High client turnover and low client retention rates make it hard to run a profitable business. But be aware that trying to have clients become dependent on you so they'll stick around actually can produce the opposite result.

"It sounds strange, but I noticed that the trainers who try to retain their clients by withholding instruction tend to anger clients and lose them quickly," says trainer

Annette Hudson. "Those clients tend to come to me. I educate them so that they will be empowered to go on their own when they are ready." A couple sessions before their package is up, she asks if they plan to continue. "If not, I can use those last sessions to prepare them to go on their own. They appreciate this and often come back a few months later for some more training."

Other causes of losing clients are:

- *Lack of results.* When clients don't see the results they want, or that they believed they were going to get, they lose interest and drop out. If this develops into a pattern, your business will not build the clientele necessary to sustain it.

- *Failing to establish goals.* Along with not getting results, it's a huge mistake when a trainer doesn't find out what a client's goals are and confirm whether they are indeed realistic and achievable. Clients with unrealistic goals are likely to drop out when they realize they aren't going to accomplish what they want.

- *Failing to maintain a sense of commitment.* Certainly clients have more in their lives than their personal fitness goals, but when the trainer is too lax and allows clients to miss sessions regularly, those clients will not make any progress and will eventually drop out.

Keeping Clients Happy

There are several simple ways to help boost your chances of keeping clients, says trainer Mike Hood. "Taking the time for the little things," he says, "is what results in retaining long-term clients." Try his suggestions:

○ If a client continues to purchase training packages, show your gratitude by giving them a free hour or a late-cancel option (allowing them one free last-minute cancellation).

○ Call a client on off-training days to see how they feel, how they are eating, or to just say hello.

○ Always be ready, smiling, motivated, and happy to see your clients. "After all," Hood says, "part of our job as a trainer is to set an example."

Don't Throw It Away

Make sure to maintain a database of contact information on former clients and prospects who went through an initial consultation and didn't sign up. In the future, you very well may want to send them a direct-mail piece and let them know about new services or special packages you're offering, as well as the addition to your staff of new trainers they may be interested in working with.

One trainer we interviewed says not keeping contact information is something he definitely regrets. "Now that I have my own studio, I'd love to send former clients and prospects a direct-mail piece and let them know what we're doing. Not keeping those records was one of my biggest mistakes."

Decide How Much You're Willing to Work

When you own the company, you can't bill every hour you work because you need to spend time running the operation, as well as training. To ward off burnout, decide in advance how many hours per week you want to work, then create a schedule and stick to it. You may work 12- to 14-hour days, plus weekends in the beginning, but that will get old fast, so don't try to do that for an extended period of time.

Avoiding Burnout

As a personal trainer, you work hard, and as with any career, you risk burnout if you don't take care of yourself. To help keep things in perspective, here are some tips.

- ○ *Have support.* Make sure you have friends or family who are there for you to talk to. Having a support system is helpful for those times when your work is draining you physically and emotionally.

- ○ *Don't neglect your own health.* You spend lots of time making sure your clients live healthy lives—just don't get so wrapped up in this pursuit that

Avoiding Burnout, continued

you don't look after your own well-being. Make time for your own work-outs and proper nutrition. Being in good physical condition and eating well give you a foundation to tackle the tough challenges you'll face as a fitness entrepreneur.

○ *Set realistic goals.* Avoid setting goals that are unrealistic or overly idealis-tic—this can set you up for disappointment.

○ *Have fun.* Don't always do the same old tired routines with your clients. Learn new exercises and training techniques and frequently change their workouts. This will challenge and improve their fitness and keep things interesting for you.

○ *Keep a balance.* Don't let your work consume your every waking hour. Cultivate hobbies and interests aside from work—and consider choosing activities that are lower pressure and not deadline driven to truly give you a break.

○ *Watch for signs.* Feeling exhausted by your work may be a sign that you're suffering from burnout. You may also lose enthusiasm for the work and eventually suffer a drop in self-esteem. Consider seeking professional help if your burnout persists.

Be Your Own Advertisement

Advertise yourself as a personal trainer whenever you are in public by wearing clothing with your company name or logo, or some other indication of what you do. Turning yourself into a walking billboard is an easy, inexpensive way to identify yourself as a personal trainer to everyone you come in contact with. T-shirts are OK, but a sharp polo-style shirt is better.

Advantages to Staying in Shape as a Trainer

It almost goes without saying that personal trainers should be a physical advertisement through looks alone for the methods they teach others, but the following list of advantages may give you some ideas for more reasons to look the part.

- Most people are attracted to toned, fit people. You'll find that people gravitate to you for a number of reasons when you're a poster child of health, and this can be good for business.

- You're more marketable for any kind of visual advertising or career expansion—including TV, film, media projects—should you decide to add these features to your career.

- It's easier to demonstrate to clients which exercises work various muscle groups when they can actually see pronounced muscles activated on your body.

- You have more energy to be a constant source of inspiration for others.

- When people see a hard, toned body, they see proof of diligent work and dedication, which instantly earns respect and gains their confidence.

- Looking in the mirror and realizing you're a product of what you believe in is a feeling like no other!

Tyrone Minor of Chizel, Inc.

Give Gifts That Come Back to You

Most personal trainers use gift-giving occasions to strengthen their relationships with clients, but birthdays, Christmas, and other holidays can also strengthen your business. Jennifer Brilliant, the personal trainer in Brooklyn, gives her clients a holiday gift each year—perhaps lotions, herbal products, or something else related to fitness—

and includes a certificate for a free session that her client can then give as a gift to someone else. "I get to meet one of their friends who they think can benefit from training," she says. "And even if that friend doesn't become a client, they've learned something about themselves, and I've had the opportunity to share my knowledge and information."

Goals and Continuing Projects

Each of the personal trainers in this book is looking forward to detailing their passions in new projects.

Tyrone Minor wants to produce a DVD series but is weighing a concern about virtual coaching. He worries that people following a DVD workout may hurt themselves without someone there to correct them if they don't understand the correct form for exercises. Though fitness DVDs usually are a good way to show form, the user has no way to make sure they are mimicking the DVD aptly without a trainer there to keep an eye on them. Minor still believes DVDs are a great addition to an in-person fitness routine, but says they can't replace an actual human being.

"People say you can't teach passion, but you can stoke the pilot light of passion into a larger flame with a little success. I try to show people that with all of the right elements they will slowly be given the reins to control their own fitness and create the body they want," Gunnar Peterson says.

Mentorship from Seasoned Experts

We asked our panel of experts the question, "What advice do you have for new personal trainers that may have helped when you were starting out?" It's smart to let someone else's hindsight be your 20-20.

Barbara Crompton's counsel is to be patient and realistic about the "glamour" of the profession. Establishing a flourishing business requires dedication and long hours, not all of which are filled with a steady stream of clientele. Belief in oneself, along with the benefits you offer others through your expertise is key, so take pride in what you do and exhibit confidence in promoting the gift of fitness you are privileged to bestow.

When we asked Diana Broschka of 501F1T what she would have done differently if she could do it all over again, she said, "I would not have opened the doors under-funded. I would've made sure we secured every dollar we needed, plus a reserve.

But, unfortunately, each investor told us . . . 'prove yourself first, then I will give you money.' Well, three and a half years into it we have proven ourselves. We've broken even and established solid partnerships and relationships. We believe we've endured the critical startup years."

Broschka laments the cost of the tradeoff and says, "However, as small business owners we have put our needs last and have endured great sacrifice on personal levels, so the next phase for us is likely to bring in a third partner to infuse capital dollars into the business to take us to the next level, including generating income as owners from the business."

Gunnar Peterson didn't plan on being a "celebrity trainer," but the fact that he operates in Beverly Hills, California, attracts that demographic. He decided that being a little famous was the only way to get the proper exposure for his powerful methods. Peterson still loves helping everyday people take control and implement methods to change their own bodies through hard work, but also has a special interest in coaching at the upper levels of fitness, such as with professional and extreme athletes.

The one downside to Salvador Mascarenas Ruiz's profession, he believes, is the lack of medical insurance, retirement benefits, and other extras that lend greater security. However, his love for what he does overrides that. He fully intends to continue teaching and training well into his later years, infusing his practice with the same dignity, class, and inspiration his professional fitness role models have demonstrated.

Appendix
Personal Training Resources

While you are an invaluable resource for your clients, we believe that you, as a trainer, can never have enough of your own resources. Therefore, we present for your consideration a wealth of sources for you to check into, check out, and harness for your own personal information blitz.

These sources are tidbits, ideas to get you started on your research. They are by no means the only sources out there, and they should not be taken as the Ultimate Answer. We have done our research, but businesses do tend to move, change, fold, and expand. As we have repeatedly stressed, do your homework. Get out and start investigating.

But keep in mind that while surfing the Net is like waltzing through a vast library, with a breathtaking array of resources literally at your fingertips, you need to use caution if you're researching health and fitness topics. Always consider the source and watch for financial or other possible biases.

Consultants and Other Experts

Robert S. Bernstein, Managing Partner, Bernstein Law Firm, P.C., Ste. 2200 Gulf Tower, 707 Grant St., Pittsburgh, PA 15219-1900, (412) 456-8101, fax: (412) 456-8251, rbernstein@bernstein law.com, www.bernsteinlaw.com

Vicki L. Helmick, CPA, 1312 Sterling Oaks Dr., Casselberry, FL 32707-3948, (407) 695-3400, fax: (407) 695-3494, vhelmick@cfl.rr.com, www.vickilhelmickcpa.com

Debbie LaChusa, The Business Stylist, PMB 310 9625 Mission Gorge Road, Suite B2, Santee, CA 92071, (619) 334-8590, www.thebizstylist.com

The Sports Management Group Inc., facility safety and risk management consulting, 1205 W. Bessemer Ave., Ste. 223, Greensboro, NC 27408, (336) 272-2071, www.smg-usa.com

Steve Tharrett, President of Club Industry Consulting, 714 Foxmoor Court, Highland Village, TX 75077, (972) 317-6703, fax: (972) 317-6703, www.clubindustryconsulting.com

Credit Card and Other Payment Processing Services

American Express Merchant Services, (800) 374-2639, www.americanexpress.com

Discover Network Card Merchant Services, (800) 347-2000, www.discovernetwork.com

MasterCard Merchant Services, www.mastercard.com

PayPal, www.paypal.com

Equipment, Supplies, and Services

Creative Health Products Inc., 7621 East Joy Rd., Ann Arbor, MI 48105, (800) 742-4478 or (734) 996-5900, fax: (734) 996-4650, www.chponline.com

Fitness Wholesale, 6333 Hudson Crossing Pkwy, Hudson, OH 44236, (800) 537-5512, fax: (800) 232-9348, www.fwonline.com

Perform Better, exercise equipment, information, and seminars for personal trainers, 11 Amflex Dr., Cranston, RI 02921, (888) 556-7464, (401) 942-9363 (international), fax: (800) 682-6950, www.performbetter.com

Sports & Fitness Insurance Corp., P.O. Box 1967, Madison, MS 39130, (800) 844-0536, fax: (601) 853-6141

SPRI Products, Inc., rubberized resistance exercise products, 1769 Northwind Blvd., Libertyville, IL 60048, (800) 222-7774, www.spriproducts.com

Fitness Organizations

Aerobics & Fitness Association of America, features certification and education, 15250 Ventura Blvd., Suite 200, Sherman Oaks, CA 91403, (877) 968-7263, www.afaa.com

American College of Sports Medicine, certification and education, P.O. Box 1440, Indianapolis, IN 46206-1440, (317) 637-9200, fax: (317) 634-7817, www.acsm.org

American Council on Exercise, certifications for fitness professionals, as well as public education on the importance of exercise, 4851 Paramount Dr., San Diego, CA 92123, (800) 825-3636, fax: (858) 565-6564, www.acefitness.com

The Cooper Institute, a research organization offering training and certification programs, 12330 Preston Rd., Dallas, TX 75230, (972) 341-3200 or (800) 635-7050, fax: (972) 341-3227, www.cooperinst.org

IDEA Health & Fitness Association, a membership organization for health and fitness professionals that features continuing education and resources but does not certify, 10455 Pacific Center Ct., San Diego, CA 92121, (800) 999-4332 or (858) 535-8979, ext. 7, fax: (858) 535-8234, www.ideafit.com

International Health, Racquet & Sportsclub Association, a member organization for health clubs, 70 Fargo St., Boston, MA 02210, (800) 228-4772 or (617) 951-0055, fax: (617) 951-0056, www.ihrsa.org

International Sports Sciences Association, offers education and certification programs, ISSA 1015 Mark Ave., Carpinteria, CA 93013, (800) 892-4772 or (805) 745-8111 (international calls), fax: (805) 745-8119, www.issaonline.com

National Academy of Sports Medicine, certifications and continuing education, 7500 W. 160th St., Stilwell, KS 66085, (800) 460-6276, fax: (913) 685-2381, www.nasm.org

National Federation of Professional Trainers, offers education and certification programs, P.O. Box 4579, Lafayette, IN 47903, (800) 729-6378, fax: (765) 471-7369, www.nfpt.com

National Strength & Conditioning Association, certification in the field of strength training and conditioning, 1885 Bob Johnson Dr., Colorado Springs, CO 80906, (719) 632-6722 or (800) 815-6826, fax: (719) 632-6367, www.nsca-lift.org

Wellcoaches, certification and education in wellness coaching, 19 Weston Rd., Wellesley, MA 02482, (866) 932-6224, www.wellcoach.com

Health-Related
Associations and Government Agencies

American Cancer Society, 250 Williams St., Atlanta, GA 30303, (800) 227-2345, www.cancer.org

American Diabetes Association, 1701 North Beauregard St., Alexandria, VA 22311, (800) 342-2383 or (703) 549-1500, www.diabetes.org

American Heart Association, 7272 Greenville Ave., Dallas, TX 75231, (800) 242-8721, www.americanheart.org

American Stroke Association, 7272 Greenville Ave., Dallas, TX 75231, (888) 478-7653, www.strokeassociation.org

Centers for Disease Control and Prevention, 1600 Clifton Rd., Atlanta, GA 30333, (800) 232-4636, www.cdc.gov

IRS, check your local telephone directory for local offices and phone numbers, www.irs.gov

National Cancer Institute, NCI Office of Communications and Education, Public Inquiries Office, 6116 Executive Blvd., Suite 300, Bethesda, MD 20892-8322, (800) 422-6237, www.cancer.gov

National Diabetes Information Clearinghouse, 1 Information Way, Bethesda, MD 20892–3560, (800) 860–8747, fax: (703) 738–4929, email: ndic@info.niddk. nih.gov, www.diabetes.niddk.nih.gov

U.S. Census Bureau, 4600 Silver Hill Rd., Washington, DC 20233, (301) 763-4636 or (800) 923-8282, www.census.gov

U.S. Copyright Office, 101 Independence Ave. SE, Washington, DC 20559-6000, (202) 707-3000 or (877) 476-0778, www.loc.gov/copyright

U.S. Food and Drug Administration (FDA), 10903 New Hampshire Ave., Silver Spring, MD 20993, (888) INFO-FDA, www.fda.gov

U.S. Patent and Trademark Office, Alexandria, VA 22313-1450, (800) 786-9199 or (571) 272-1000, www.uspto.gov

The Weight-Control Information Network, 1 WIN Wy., Bethesda, MD 20892-3665, (877) 946-4627 or (202) 828-1025, fax: (202) 828-1028, http://win.niddk. nih.gov/

Magazines, Books, and Other Publications

American Council on Exercise (ACE), 4851 Paramount Dr., San Diego, CA 92123, (858) 576-6500 or (888) 825-3636, fax: (858) 576-6564, www.acefitness.com

American College of Sports Medicine, various free brochures, P.O. Box 1440, Indianapolis, IN 46206-1440, (317) 637-9200, fax: (317) 634-7817, www.acsm.org

Club Industry's Fitness Business Pro, a monthly magazine for owners and operators of commercial health and fitness facilities, 9800 Metcalf Ave., Overland Park, KS 66212, (913) 341-1300, www.clubindustry.com

IDEA Fitness Journal and IDEA Trainer Success, publications produced by IDEA, 10455 Pacific Center Ct., San Diego, CA 92121, (800) 999-4332, ext. 7, or (858) 535-8979, ext. 7, fax: (858) 535-8234, www.ideafit.com

G-Werx Workout Program Guide by Phil Martens, 501 S. Washington Ave., 3rd Flr., Minneapolis, MN 55415, (612) 767-4415, www.501fit.com

"The Obesity Epidemic: A Confidence Crisis Calling for Professional Coaches," Wellcoaches White Paper, accessible at www.wellcoaches.com/ images/whitepaper.pdf

Strength and Conditioning Journal and The Journal of Strength and Conditioning Research, publications of National Strength & Conditioning Association, 1885 Bob Johnson Dr., Colorado Springs, CO 80906, (800) 815-6826 or (719) 632-6722 or (800) 815-6826, fax: (719) 632-6367, www.nsca-lift.org

Miscellaneous Resources

Club Industry Show, (866) 513-0767 or (708) 486-0767, registration@penton.com, www.clubindustryshow.com

Fitness Together, personal training franchise company, 9092 Ridgeline Blvd. Ste. A, Highlands Ranch, CO 80129, (877) 663-0880, fax: (303) 663-1617

Institute for Credentialing Excellence (ICE), an organization that sets quality standards for credentialing organizations, 2025 M St. NW, Suite 800, Washington, DC 20036, (202) 367-1165, fax: (202) 367-2165, www.credentialingexcellence.org

National Commission for Certifying Agencies (NCCA), the accreditation body of ICE, www.credentialingexcellence.org

PR Newswire, media and PR resources, 350 Hudson St., Suite 300, New York, NY 10014, (866) 641-4636, www.prnewswire.com

Performing Rights Organizations

The American Society of Composers, Authors and Publishers, One Lincoln Plaza, New York, NY 10023, (800) 505-4052, www.ascap.com

Broadcast Music, Inc., 7 World Trade Center, 250 Greenwich St., New York, NY 10007-0030, (212) 220-3000, www.bmi.com

SESAC, 55 Music Square E., Nashville, TN 37203, (615) 320-0055, fax: (615) 321-6292, www.sesac.com

Social Media Experts

Chris Brogan, www.chrisbrogan.com

Khoa Bui, Khoa Bui International, 243/1 Heritage Cove, Maylands 6051, Western Australia, (08) 6102 1277, www.khoa-bui.com, support@khoa-bui.com

Guy Kawasaki, www.guykawasaki.com, kawasaki@garage.com

Shannon Paul, (734) 968-9065, shannonpaul5@gmail.com, www.veryofficialblog.com

Gary Vaynerchuk, www.garyvaynerchuk.com, www.vaynermedia.com, 220 E 23rd Street, Suite 605, New York, NY 10010, info@vaynermedia.com

Software and Web-Based Tools and Services

Aspen Information Systems Inc., fitness assessment software, P.O. Box 680031, Houston, TX 77268, (800) 414-0343 or (281) 320-0343, www.aspensoftware.com

BSDI, assessment, training and client retention software, Box 357, Califon, NJ 07830, (888) 273-4348 or (908) 832-2691 (international), fax: (909) 832-2670, www.bsdiweb.com

Gubb.net, online list sharing, www.gubb.net

Guru.com, project bidding website, 5001 Baum Blvd., Suite 760, Pittsburgh, PA 15213, (888) 678-0136, fax: (412) 687-4466, www.guru.com

Network Solutions, domain registration services, www.networksolutions.com

Register.com, web hosting, www.register.com, (800) 734-4783

Sitesell.com, web hosting and promotion, www.sitesell.com, (866) 281-2789

Vesteon Software, 8739 Bandera Rd., Suite 133–155, San Antonio, TX 78250, (210) 325-8982, www.vesteon-software.com

WebFlexor Technologies, online training tools, 1010 University Ave., #1685, San Diego, CA 92103-3395, (888) 282-7818, www.hitechtrainer.com and www.hitechwebflexor.com

Wellcoaches, 19 Weston Rd., Wellesley, MA 02482, (866) 932-6224, www.wellcoach.com

www.motionsoft.net

Successful Personal Trainers

501F1T, Phil Martens and Diana Broschka, Owners, 501 S. Washington Ave., 3rd Floor, Minneapolis, MN 55415, (612) 767-4415, info@501fit.com, www.501fit.com, www.gwerx.com

Jennifer Brilliant, Jennifer Brilliant Yoga and Personal Training, LLC, 732A Carroll St., Brooklyn, NY 11215, (718) 499-7282, Jennifer@JenniferBrilliant.com, www.JenniferBrilliant.com

Louis Coraggio, Body Architect, (516) 768-0889, info@bodyarch.com, www.bodyarch.com

Richard T. Cotton, MA, chief exercise physiologist, MyExercisePlan.com and Executive Wellness Coach, richard@richardcotton.com, (760) 930-4090

Barbara Crompton, CEO, Graham Group and Yoga Teacher, 20191972 Robson St., Vancouver, Canada V6G1E8 and Mex 584 Cuahahtomec, Puerto Vallarta, Mexico, (604) 618-4591, www.barbaracrompton.com

Ellen G. Goldman, M.Ed., EnerG Coaching, LLC—Fitness & Wellness from the Inside Out, (973) 535-8891, ellen@energcoaching.com, www.EnerGcoaching.com

Pat Henry, owner, instructor, Organic Stretching™, 2163 Lima Loop, Suite 130-362, Laredo, TX 78045, (210) 399-7214 and Las Glorias #6, Colonia Jose Chavez, La Cruz de Huanacaxtle, Nayarit, Mexico, (329) 295-5289, www.pat-henry.com/organicstretching

Mike Hood, Mike Hood Fitness, New York City, NY, (646) 288-2035, www.linkedin.com/in/mikehoodfit

Annette Hudson, creator of www.MyFitnessTrainer.com, P.O. Box 731295, Puyallup, WA 98373, info@myfitnesstrainer.com

Fabiola Noemi Marcial, zumba instructor, Aguacate 573 Colonia Alta Vista, Puerto Vallarta, Jalisco, Mexico, 044-322 160 5720, fabylopez_69@hotmail.com

Tyrone Minor, Chizel Inc., (612) 916-0930, www.chizelinc.com

Gunnar Peterson, 9663 Santa Monica Blvd., Suite 849, Beverly Hills, CA 90210, Gunnar9@earthlink.net, www.gunnarpeterson.com

Salvador Mascarenas Ruiz, workout trainer, 380 Tenth St., San Francisco, CA 94103, (322) 222-5573 and 517 Jacarandas St., Suite 101, Alta Vista, Puerto Vallarta, Mexico 48300, 044-322-135-5847, Salvadormascarena@yahoo.com

Bill Sonnemaker, founder and CEO of Catalyst Fitness, 404 Ponce de Leon Place NE, Atlanta, GA 30306, (404) 856-0513, info@catalystfitness.com, www.catalystfitness.com

Lynne Wells, lynne@wellbodyfit.com, www.wellbodyfit.com

Useful Websites

www.affirmativefitness.com, an online directory of personal trainers

www.ars.usda.gov/main/site_main.htm?modecode=12354500, the USDA's Nutrient Data Laboratory, where you can search for nutrient breakdowns of specific foods

www.hsph.harvard.edu/nutritionsource, information from the Department of Nutrition of the Harvard School of Public Health

www.mayoclinic.com, the Mayo Clinic's information on diseases and conditions

www.medlineplus.com, a medical dictionary and encyclopedia, helpful links to other resources, maintained by the U.S. National Library of Medicine and the National Institutes of Health

www.mypyramid.gov, the federal government's site for its food guide pyramid, including an interactive tool that personalizes the pyramid's recommendations

www.ods.od.nih.gov/index.aspx, information on supplements from the Office of Dietary Supplements of the National Institutes of Health

www.pubmed.gov, a service of the National Library of Medicine and the National Institutes of Health, where you can search a database of thousands of journals for studies on health, diet, and exercise—you'll find abstracts plus many free full-text articles

www.realage.com, gives you an estimate of your biological age compared to your calendar age

www.webmd.com, featuring health news and guides

www.womenshealth.gov, covers health topics for women from the U.S. Department of Health & Human Services

Glossary

BarWorks: an exercise practice combining yoga, ballet, and pilates using specific alignment principles from the YogaWorks (www.yogaworks.com) method

Behavioral contract: a written agreement to yourself or another to behave in a prescribed manner.

Body Mass Index (BMI): a relative measure of body weight to body height; for most people this correlates closely with body fat. The number is calculated by dividing weight (in pounds) by height squared (in inches) and then multiplying by 703. A BMI of 30 or more is considered obese by U.S. standards.

Boot camp: got its name from military basic training but in the fitness world refers to group training and most often involves running, weights, and interval drills, usually in an outdoor setting.

Capoeria: a Brazilian art form that combines elements of martial arts, sports, and music.

Centers for Disease Control and Prevention (CDC): an agency composed of a number of centers, institutes, and offices that aims to promote health and quality of life by preventing and controlling disease, injury, and disability.

▲

Certification: the act of attesting that an individual or organization has met a specific set of standards; fitness certifications are established by organizations within the fitness industry.

Core training: strength training focusing on the back, stomach, and shoulders with proper alignment, defined "six pack" muscles, and injury prevention as some of its benefits.

Cortisol: a steroid hormone produced by the adrenal gland, also known as the "stress hormone," because it is activated when the body is stressed.

CPR: cardiopulmonary resuscitation.

CSCS certification: strength and conditioning instructor certification created by the NCSA (National Strength and Conditioning Association), which focuses on strength training and conditioning to improve athletic performance.

Empathy: understanding another person's point of view in a manner that still allows objective reasoning.

Environmental Protection Agency (EPA): a government agency with the mission of protecting human health and safeguarding the natural environment.

Epidemiology: the study of distribution and determinants of diseases or other health outcomes in human populations.

Exercise physiologist: a scientist who conducts controlled investigations of responses and adaptations to muscular activity using human subjects or animals within a clinical, research, or academic setting; exercise physiologists are degreed and certified in exercise physiology or a related field.

Exercise prescription: a physician's recommendation or referral for exercise; the recommended volume of exercise including frequency, intensity, duration, and type of exercise.

Fitness evaluation: a series of tests designed to assess cardiovascular fitness, body-fat percentage, flexibility, and muscular strength and endurance.

Food and Drug Administration (FDA): the regulatory agency that is part of the Public Health Service of the U.S. Department of Health and Human Services; responsible for ensuring the safety and wholesomeness of all foods sold in interstate commerce (except meat, poultry, and eggs).

Food and Nutrition Board (FNB): established in 1940 under the National Academy of Sciences to study issues pertaining to the safety and adequacy of the nation's food supply; establish principles and guidelines for adequate nutrition; and render authoritative judgment on the relationships among food intake, nutrition, and health at the request of various agencies.

General liability insurance: insurance covering the insured for bodily injury or property damage resulting from general negligence.

GRAS: an acronym for "generally recognized as safe."

HTML: stands for HyperText Markup Language and is the predominant language, or building block system, of most web pages and is behind the scenes creating what viewers see on websites.

Independent contractors: individuals who conduct business independently on a contract basis and are not employees of an organization or business.

Informed consent: voluntary acknowledgment of the purpose, procedures, and specific risks of an activity in which one intends to engage.

International Food Information Council (IFIC): a nonprofit association supported by food, beverage, and agricultural companies to assist the media, educators, health professionals, and scientists to effectively communicate science-based information on health, nutrition, and food safety.

Kinesiology: the study of human movement.

Liability: legal responsibility.

Modeling: the process of learning by observing and imitating others' behavior.

National Health and Nutrition Examination Survey (NHANES): a series of surveys that include information from medical history, physical measurements, biochemical evaluation, physical examination, and dietary intake of population groups within the United States conducted by the U.S. Department of Health and Human Services approximately every five years.

Nationwide Food Consumption Survey (NFCS): a survey conducted by the USDA roughly every ten years that monitors nutrient intake of a cross section of the U.S. public.

Permalink: a URL, or web address link, that points to a specific blog or article/entry after it has passed through the homepage, and remains unchanged indefinitely.

Personalized exercise program: an individualized exercise program based on the person's fitness evaluation results, and personal fitness and health goals.

Professional liability insurance: insurance covering the insured for damages resulting from negligence, errors, or omissions.

▲

Sciatica: a common form of leg and low back pain or numbness caused by weakness or injury to the sciatica nerve.

U.S. Department of Agriculture (USDA): the government department comprised of numerous agencies charged with different tasks related to agriculture and the food supply.

Waiver: voluntary abandonment of a right to file suit; not always legally binding.

Weight-control Information Network (WIN): an information service of the National Institute of Diabetes and Digestive and Kidney Diseases of the National Institutes of Health; assembles and disseminates information on weight control, obesity, and nutritional disorders to health professionals and the general public.

Index

▲